W9-DJN-543

5

Warrior
Poets
and
Warrior
Saints

Nannette Morrison

WITHDRAWN
by Unity Library

UNITY SCHOOL LIBRARY
UNITY VILLAGE, MISSOURI 64065

Echo Effects Publishing

Books by Nannette Morrison

Echoes of Valor

~

A Thundering Silence

~

Warrior Poets and Warrior Saints

11/00

Warrior Poets, Warrior Saints

Copyright © 1998 by Nannette Morrison
All rights reserved under the International and Pan-American Copyright Convention. No part of this book may be reproduced in any form, or by any means, without the written permission from the publisher.

Published by
Echo Effects Publishing
1310 Lester Drive
Charlottesville, VA 22901
804-293-9650
http://www.cstone.net/~cmillard/warrior.htm

ISBN 0-9663108-2-9

Manufactured in the United States of America

Contents

D
70
M6
1998
C.1

Foreword

The Celts were tribes of people—Bretons, Irish, Gaels or British—shifting through periods of time in adaptation. As we still are. They had a Destiny which they bequeathed to us. That was their love for life and uncanny knack of getting us to look at the mystery of things…the feel of something spiritual and a fierce call to personal independence and freedom.

A Celtic Soul is deeply committed to the continuance of life. Thus we are given the Celtic Knot as this symbol. Through their song, poetry, myths and magical tradition, the passion of their lives and insights into the very depths of human life are made clearer to us who have, to some extent, lost that connection. These remarkable people could make something of beauty from tragedy.

The "Pagan" Celts believed in a pantheon of gods, supernatural 'other-world'; all aspects of Nature were sacred to them. Through their colorful and imaginative system of mythology, all sacred articles were revered and kept alive. Within these beliefs and ceremonies, lie the very roots of Christianity, not a threat to nor a contradiction of it. The symbols, colors, and ceremonies of Easter, May Day, Sundays, and Communion are but a few examples.

There remain those true great guardians of tradition, those immortals whose memory serves to restore the history of the ages to their successors. In some form C. Jung would have referred to them as archetypes. Fortunately, the marvelous memories of these guardians have been passed down to the bards and poets of Scotland and Ireland.

Combining this with their undeniable passion and commitment to all that is meaningful, the Celts were and remain some of the greatest warriors, as well as poets, that ever lived. In our 'modern, technical' world of today, Love for Life is slowly slipping away...would that we all inherit the Souls of the Saints and Poets.

Prologue

"The Minstrel Boy to the war is gone,
 in the ranks of death you'll find him,
His father's sword he has girded on,
And his wild harp hung behind him.
"Land of Song," said the Warrior Bard
"Tho, all the world betrays thee,
One sword at least thy Right shall guard,
One faithful Harp shall praise thee."

Angus sat listening intently to the youthful, lilting Irish voice. Its clear sound made chills race up and down his spine. Angus perched on a comfortable rock, possibly the same boulder that Reverend Corby climbed up on to give absolution to the Irish Brigade that second day of July, 1863.

The man's imagination transported him back to that day as the crash of cannister reverberated through the woods and smoke enveloped the nearby forest. From their position at Cemetery Ridge, Angus pictured the men of the Fighting Irish waiting for their orders to attack.

Yet, the lyrics of "The Minstrel Boy" were quite real; nor by far was this the first morning he'd sat patiently listening, but never seeing the soldier.

Angus had a lengthy career as a photographer for "National Geographic Magazine" behind him. He'd made himself a promise ages ago, that when he retired, he would move to Gettysburg. Then he would have the leisure time to walk the battlefield and to film it, hopefully to capture some of its elusive, wispy figures from the past.

Thus far, Angus had seen no success with his cameras. He eased himself down from the rock. It was still early enough to catch dawn's atmosphere. He ambled away southward, in the direction of Devil's Den.

Oddly enough, the farther he walked, the thicker the fog became. Angus experienced pangs of nervous energy as he drew nearer to Devil's Den. He realized that his own footsteps had softened while he neared the impressive rock clusters. Then they halted.

A Scottish bagpipe's plaintiff skirl reached Angus' ears. Strains of the lament, "Women of the Glen," drifted through the heavy mist. Angus' blood froze like ice as he stood there mesmerized, waiting, hoping for the lazy mists to clear.

For Angus the next several seconds seemed like a lifetime. The swirling mists parted atop the den. Before him majestically stood a Highland piper in full regalia of tartan plaids, sporran and pipes. As though in slow motion, the Highlander turned to stare directly at Angus whose heart suddenly skipped a beat. Only then was he aware of warm tears streaming down his cheeks.

"Some memories are forever, and the memory of the living is the dwelling place of the dead," the Highlander said. Then he was gone.

Ghostly image of woman dressed in mourning sitting atop Devil's Den. As Susan Wright of Colonial Heights took the photograph September of 1996, there was no one visible until the film was developed.

Hammer of the Scots

"From the devil they came, and to the devil they shall return," was the phrase often repeated referring to the Plantagenet family. The family name Platagenet derives from the "Planta genista," a sprig of broom worn in the helmets of the fearless Dukes of Anjou in battle.

This dynasty was linked throughout its dark Angevin history with deep roots of witchcraft and was apparently born from a long line of pagans. Fulk the Black was the first of the line with such evil and cruel character that their House would then carry that fatal brand through 200 years.

Henry II is remembered chiefly for ordering the murder of Becket, the Archbishop of Canterbury, in 1170. Henry II fathered two sons, Richard and John, in whom the characteristics of unbridled cruelty and violent temper raged supremely.

John rose to the English throne in 1199 and began a horrible reign of terror. In 1212 King John personally hanged 28 young boys at Nottingham Court. These had been the youngest child of each of his most powerful barons, given up as hostage to ensure their good behavior towards John. One outrage followed another during the grasping and deceitful reign of King John.

His favorite method of death for his victims, mothers and children, as well as knights, was starvation. But John was also known for the death of Arthur of Britain who died of shock and blood loss as the King had him blinded and castrated.

William de Braose, one of the most powerful barons, was beside himself with anger and grief at the King's murder by starvation in a dungeon of de Braose's wife and son. He finally called down all the demonic hell he could summon upon John's head. "I call upon the Damned to likewise damn the Bramber Woods of Suosexe, and may John and his creed n'er walk in peace".

Henry III, John's son, was quite unremarkable as a ruler. His actions and decisions were never adhered to long enough to be deemed reliable. However, he fathered the man who would be remembered as the Hammer of the Scots.

Edward I had a brush with greatness; unfortunately he let it pass him by. During his early years as King, he had an ideal of including the common people in the decisions of the government. He created the two houses of the first Parliament, consisting of the House of Lords and the House of Commons. However, as he aged, Edward lost interest in this vision. Above all he firmly believed in his Divine Right to rule.

In 1284 Edward launched into his first military conquest and defeated the Welsh. By 1290 Margaret, the Maid of Norway, the direct heir to the Scottish throne had died, leaving their people in dispute involving the many contenders for the crown. Out of desperation the citizens of Scotland called on Edward as mediator. Edward, however, saw this as an acknowledgment of his overlordship. He quickly began to assume powers over Scottish affairs that alarmed the regency. He now acted as though all decisions concerning Scotland were his responsibility alone.

Edward was about to make his first serious mistake. He assumed that he could subdue the Scots as readily as he had the Welsh. His second disastrous mistake would be underestimating the tenacity and fierceness of the Scottish people.

Edward chose Berwick to launch his attack versus the citizens of Scotland. At the time Berwick-on-Tweed was the center of the wool trade, as well as Scotland's chief seaport and center for shipbuilding. Still, it was poorly fortified, while Edward's preparations for its invasion was thorough.

As the English troops approached, the people of Berwick sat on the earth-on-wood fortifications and jeered at the King. They dubbed him "Edward Longshanks." This sent Edward, mounted on his favorite horse Bayard, over Berwick's walls in a black fury. England's formidable war machine barely met with any resistance. Once the city was conquered, Edward ordered the mass execution of all its male citizens. Almost immediately the citizens were given over to the passions of the King's soldiers. The descriptions of the atrocities seen that day are those of barbarous cruelties. Midst Berwick's sea of blood, Longshanks created one of the most shameful pages in English history.

Estimates of the Scots who perished that day range from 17,000 to 60,000. The dead lay piled in the streets and hanging from windows for days before they were thrown into the sea or buried in mass pits.

News of the sack of Berwick moved as shock-waves throughout Scotland, firing up the Scots with a zeal previously unknown. This tactical mistake of Berwick on the part of England's king would soon bring forth Scotland's most legendary warrior, William Wallace, his country's champion of liberty.

Monument to William Wallace atop Abbey Craig

Scots on the Ascendant

After Berwick Edward rode across Scotland treating it as though it was a conquered country. He deposed King John Balliol, the Scots' 'appointed' ruler, in the most humiliating manner possible. Hostages were taken and sent south to England while Edward required oaths of fealty known as the Ragman Roll. Scottish records were confiscated, as well as regalia and the Stone of Destiny on which every Scottish King had been enthroned.

Scotland had a bardic tradition of word-of-mouth, of minstrels moving from one great hall to another with tales of past battles and invincible heroes, telling stirring tales much of which would otherwise be lost forever. For this we must thank Blind Harry and others like him who preserved the tales of heroes', exploits to be enshrined in the hearts and memories of Scots around the world.

Scot's anger over English occupation was on the ascendant.. There appeared from the wilds of Scotland a fearless rebel of such passion that would raise the country's spirit of independence to new heights. In the winter of 1296 William Wallace raised his head.

The Wallace family motto was 'Esperance', meaning 'Hope'; and according to Blind Harry, was 'of whole lineage and true line of Scotland'. An active supporter of Robert the Bruce, William's grandfather was Sheriff of Ayr in 1296. William was one of two sons of Sir Malcom Wallace of Elderslie.

William was fearless and brave from birth to the grave. Yet, a number of factors entered into the making of his further determination to free his people from English dominion. His father Sir Malcolm was a courageous knight who refused to obey Edward. As a result Malcolm died at the hands of Fenwick, an English officer, in 1296.

Sir Malcolm's brother also played a major role in young Wallace's development. 'Freedom is best, I tell thee true, of all things to be won. Then never live within the bond of slavery,' was his uncle's favorite expression, passing it on to be the same for William. But the price of Freedom is often quite dear.

In about 1296 William married Marion (Mirren) Bradfute of Lamington. Together, they produced a daughter. To Mirren's demise, she was jealously admired by Heselrig the Sheriff of Lanark. It was prearranged that the Sheriff's cronies would force Wallace into a scuffle, to end in his death. Mirren aided in his escape, but died as a result by the hand of Heselrig.

Murders of the two people closest to Wallace only served to harden his resolve against the English. In early May 1297, Heselrig would pay with his own life for Mirren's murder. Scottish patriots began flocking to Wallace's side. His charisma, handsome physical features, unusually tall stature, and physical power made Wallace an easy man to follow. His passion in decision making and actions would soon prove to extract an uncanny loyalty from thousands of Scots.

It was True Thomas the Rimer, a reputable prophet of the day, who predicted of Wallace that he would be the one who would drive the English out of Scotland. The wheels were set in motion and the scene was set for this to happen. One of the features of Scotland which aided the rebellion was the great tract of forest over southern Scotland into which Wallace and his men could disappear and hide. Its forests stretched for immense distances interspersed with moors, boglands or ravines. From the wilds of the Selkirk woods, Wallace trained his men and began launching those guerrilla attacks which enabled his troops to be so effective. The Scottish fighting tradition of warfare was on foot, especially since the Highlands, braes, and marches were not conducive to battle from horseback.

The English knights, by contrast, were highly trained professionals accustomed to battle from the vantage point atop heavy destriers. These members of the English heavy cavalry were notably well-financed to equip them and to keep their skills to a level of excellence.

The hobelars or light cavalry were to prove somewhat more vulnerable against the Scots. The appearance of the Welsh longbow and the Scottish schiltrons would reshape the maneuvers of the War of Independence.

Adding further fuel to the embers of Berwick, was Edward's determination to anglicize the Scottish Church. The Catholic Church in Scotland considered this interference an outrage and an outright attempt by England's King to undermine the very roots of Scottish life. Edward was also taking on the wrath, as well as the influence of the Scottish Church.

What began as annoying disturbances through the winter of 1296, developed into full scale uprisings in the spring of 1297. To the north another young patriot Andrew de Moray was designing a twin campaign to Wallace's. Together in 1297 the two warriors would share the joint Guardianship of Scotland.

Andrew, a kinsman to the powerful Comyns of the north country, was a young knight taken prisoner after the fight at Dunbar. His father eventually died in the Tower, but Andrew was sent to Chester Castle. Edward was wary of this Celtic family. Not only did they hold vast lands in Scotland, but they had important connections to the Church of Scotland.

Andrew escaped from Chester Castle, probably through the aid of Bishop Wishart, and headed for his family's stronghold north of Inverness. Similar to Wallace, men from all over joined de Moray's army. His forays against the English were amazingly similar to Wallace's tactics. While Wallace rallied the southern Scots, Andrew raised the banner of freedom to the north and was devastating every English-held fortification in his path.

Urquhart Castle upon its isolated, impressive position overlooking Lock Ness wasn't just a fortress. It proclaimed the power of lordship over the people of the glen. As a result of Berwick's fall, Edward had advanced northward and had taken Urquhart Castle. However, because of its distance from England, it was difficult for them to retain. De Moray planned a night attack on Urquhart in late July, 1297, taking Sir William Fitzwarine its constable by surprise and laying siege to its garrisons.

The English's tentative grip on Scotland was methodically being pried loose. Andrew was enjoying such victories to the north in country familiar to him and seemed reluctant to join forces with Wallace southward. In response to Bishop Wishart's appeal for the two forces to combine, Wallace headed north and then east.

Ardrossan Castle in Ayrshire standing on a ridge called Castle Hill overlooking the harbour fell to Wallace's attack during one of these excursions. The English garrison resisted and Wallace had them slaughtered, then tossed into its dungeon. Wallace's Larder, as it is known, is quite alive today with William's spirit. On stormy, rainy nights, his powerful frame can still be seen wielding his 5'7" claymore or 'claidheamh dà làimh.'

Edward, often compared to a leopard, considered a devious animal during the thirteenth century, was again incensed. Wallace had just destroyed a large quantity of English shipping in Aberdeen. Cressingham and Warenne's forces linked together to squash the Scots' uprising. Now, the combined English forces included a thousand horse and 50,000 infantry. They left Berwick to venture northwards in pursuit of the obstinate rebels.

The two markedly different armies were destined to meet at Stirling Bridge. The area was dominated by nearby Stirling Castle, whose river crossing was the most strategically vital in Scotland.

"The sword that seemed fit for an Archangel to wield was light in his terrible hand"—William Wallace fought at Stirling Bridge, Sept. 11, 1305. Photo of Wallace's sword on display in Wallace Monument.

Main courtyard of Stirling Castle

Stirling Castle

Stirling is one of the most powerful castles in Scotland. It is a courtyard castle, standing on a high rock, looking clearly out in many directions. It is more than possible that its location was chosen carefully for more esoteric reasons than military importance. Stirling Castle is one of the many structures placed on the powerful ley-lines running through the earth. This phenomenon by which prehistoric mounds, churches, castles, etc. appear to lie on a straight line holds important magnetic energy . Stirling Castle, Ben Lomond, Rob Roy's Prison, Arrochar, Inverary, and Iona lie on what is referred to as the 'old straight track to Iona.'

As Elizabeth and I walked quietly atop the castle's high walls, I could smell the flowery presence of a waif from many years ago. No flowers were in bloom midst the courtyard garden that day late in October. "What did you say?" Elizabeth asked me to repeat my words, as I approached from the nearby turret.

"Nothing," was my reply. "I wasn't talking at all."

She assumed a mysterious look, "Oh really. Well I was just standing here listening to women's voices, muffled, but carried to me through the ages." October is a month of very few tourists and none were around that day.

Parts of Castle Stirling date to the 12th century . The 'King's Old Building' contained royal chambers, and the 'Chapel Royal' was the location of the crowning of Mary, Queen of Scots in 1533. In 1124 Alexander I died behind its walls. December 1174 it became garrisoned by English troops after William the Lyon was forced to sign a treaty with King Henry. William the Lyon would also come to his death in the castle in 1214.

King Henry III of England caused more trouble for his northern neighbors. He and his supporters effected the capture of Margaret and Alexander of Scotland in 1254. The Comyns, however, managed to rescue the pair in 1257 and placed them safely in Stirling Castle.

By April 27, 1296 the Scots were again trying to withstand English dominion. The Scottish army took their stand near Dunbar, but were totally defeated. Several castle garrisons surrendered in the wake of Edward I. When he reached Stirling's gates, its garrison had already fled.

Later in 1304, Edward would again capture the castle. Then, typical of his character, he employed his terrible siege engine—the 'War Wolf' —even after the garrison had laid down arms.

Much history continued to parade through Stirling's walls. In 1452 James II murdered the 8th Earl of Douglas, tossing his body out one of the windows overlooking a small garden in a rear courtyard. Some people speculate that it's the Earl's wife, currently referred to as the Pink Lady, who seeks her husband. The Pink Lady is the apparition of a beautiful woman in a pink silk gown seen around Stirling Castle. Other people seem to feel that she is the wife of one of the men killed as Edward attacked the garrison. As she drifts along in her tall finery, the Lady in Pink also resembles Mary, Queen of Scots.

What is thought to be one of Queen Mary's ladies-in-waiting, the specter called the 'Green Lady,' is usually associated with fire. This lady saved the Queen's life once when her bedclothes caught fire. Dozens of people see and hear the moaning spirit of this same 'Green Lady.' They also believe her to be a pretty teenage girl who died of heartbreak soon after her fiancé was killed by an arrow while on sentry duty as part of the castle's garrison. The 'Green Lady' has often been seen recently.

The church of Dunipace, connected with Cambuskenneth Abby, was close by Stirling Castle to its east. The River Forth wound around snakelike between the town and Abbey Craig with Tor Wood. Stirling Castle perched regally overlooking all and forever the connecting link between Scotland's lowlands and highlands. This day of 1297 history at Stirling Castle would again be written.

Stirling Bridge

The morning of September 11, 1297 dawned clear as the autumn sun glinted off the River Forth. Much earlier the English force started across the wooden bridge, only to be recalled because Warenne had overslept. This attempt, however, would be different. This would be William Wallace's opportunity to prove his genius on the battlefield.

With a clear picture of the terrain between the town of Sterling and the wooded area leading up to the Abby Craig, William and Andrew hid their men in tense silence. For nearly two hours Celtic hearts pounded as they watched the powerful English army advance toward them - fearsome mailed knights with plumed helmets, colorful banners fluttering, experienced spearmen, horses neighing in agitation, men's shouts of orders, the tramping of foot soldiers, and dreaded Welsh archers.

It says much of the loyalty and obedience of Wallace's men to wait patiently, undetected while these troops maneuvered Stirling Bridge. Eleven o'clock Wallace sounded the attack from Abbey Craig with a single blast on his horn.

Yelling their clan battle cries and calling on Saint Margaret, the Scots poured towards the river. "On them!" On them!" they shouted, urging each other on.

The English heavy cavalry north of the bridge was cut to pieces. One-hundred knights were slain and their mounts' bellies cut open or hamstrung. Others threw off their armour attempting to swim to safety. But, this day Celtic blood was irresistible. Horses floundered in the thick mud, taking their warriors down with them. Warenne fled from the scene, but the arrogant Cressingham was not so fortunate to survive the melée. Wallace's men fought with a raw energy, the revenge for Berwick heavy in their memories. Still the English force yet uncommitted to the bridge lined the river bank. As they watched the nightmare before them, they realized that these Celtic devils did not fight as ordinary men. English resolve diminished as the remaining forces filtered away.

De Moray was severely wounded, not only a loss for Scotland but a serious one for Wallace. The chivalric co-leader was carried to his homelands where he died two months later. But before he died, Andrew shared joint Guardianship of Scotland with Wallace. The full burden of military leadership now fell on William's shoulders.

The Battle of Stirling Bridge altered the possibilities of war. It proved that under certain circumstances, an army of foot soldiers can defeat one of armoured cavalry. Nevertheless, it did not end the war.

Urquhart Castle

Urquhart Castle, with its breathtaking views, stands on a rugged and irregular promontory jutting into the icy waters of Loch Ness. Throughout its 500-year history, Urquhart Castle has endured much warlike activity and particularly figured prominently in the Scots' struggle for independence

One furiously windy day in October, I sat midst her Great Hall and received information from a messenger reappearing from ancient ages. The image was garbed as a warrior, yet not one of a fully mailed knight. He crossed Urquhart's moat, mounted on a bay garron. The man, who I now believe to be Andrew de Moray, left me with a message. That message was the inspiration for "Warrior Poets and Warrior Saints."

St. Columba came from the warrior aristocracy and patently had an abiding personal interest in battles. During his life well before his death in 597, Columba traveled from his Celtic home in Dal Riata, of western Scottish lands, to visit a Pictish King named Brude. Lands directly beside Loch Ness were the location of Brude's residence. An elderly gentleman named Emchath also played host in Glen Urquhart to Columba and his fellow monks during this same visit. It was at this time that Columba converted Emchath and his family to Christianity.

The discovery of a piece of Pictish brooch midst the ruins of Urquhart Castle has led to speculation that it was the site of the home

Urquhart Castle overlooking Lock Ness

of either Emchath or Brude. Evidence of a well-defended hill-fort constructed in the first millennium A.D. can be found on the slopes of the craggy summit of the upper bailey. Pieces of vitrified stone, from rampart walls that had been subjected to intense heat, have been discovered over the years. Evidence from radio-carbon dating fully supports this too.

The province of Moray had its own banner -'Vexillum Moraviae.' Moray differed from other earldoms by reason of a large number of men known as "the freemen of Moray" who held their lands on condition that they gave the King military aid. The people of Moray essentially owed no feudal superior other than the monarch.

In 1228 the independent-minded people of this huge province revolted against their King Alexander II. This revolution, however, was crushed. Alan Durward, the King's son-in-law, was granted the first lordship of Urquhart. This was established along with others of the King's men being relocated north on orders to hold the area secure. Most certainly Durward needed an impregnable fortress to secure his estate against the surrounding hostile population. This first castle was probably centered on the summit of the upper bailey. On the landward side, Urquhart Castle was defended by a large rock-cut ditch. Outwardly and inwardly, it was a most secure defense position for its inhabitants because of the strategic military position.

Upon Alan Durward's death in 1275, the Urquhart estates were granted to John Comyn 'the Red,' Lord of Badenoch and Lochaber. It was garrisoned in 1296 with English forces of Edward I. Then in summer of 1297 was Andrew de Moray's attack against the fortress. As a result of Andrew's onslaught, Edward issued orders that the castle be, "so strengthened and garrisoned that no damage in any way may occur to it." Apparently, these orders were not seen through.

A story recorded by a contemporary of Wallace and Robert the Bruce, who happened to be residing at Urquhart Castle at the time, tells of one of William's encounters with the English. "The area then called 'Wallaceslack' was the locale along where the English troops chose to march in order to join more of their own. The eminence overtopping the ravine provided an excellent ambush point for Wallace. His strategy succeeded. The English, much surprised and panic-stuck, were defeated with six-hundred dead."

Another of Scotland's humble poets composed lines in 1846 praising Wallace's success at Urquhart Castle:

> Thus ran the tale:—proud England's host
> Lay 'trench'd on Croma's winding coast,
> And rose the Urquhart's towers beneath
> Fierce shouts of wars, deep groans of death.
> The Wallace heard;—from Moray's shore
> One little bark his warriors bore,
> But died the breeze, and rose the day,
> Ere gain'd that bark the destined bay;
> When, lo! these rocks a quay supplied,
> These yawning caves meet shades to hide.
> Secure, where rank the nightshade grew,
> And patter'd thick th' unwholesome dew,
> Patient of cold and gloom they lay,
> Till eve's last light had died away.
>
> It died away;—in Croma's hall
> No flame glanced on the trophied wall,
> Nor sound of mirth nor revel free
> Was heard where joy had wont to be.
> With day had ceased the siege's din,
> But still gaunt famine raged within.
>
> In chamber lone, on weary bed,
> That castle's wounded lord was laid;
> His woe-worn lady watch'd beside.
> To pain devote, and grief, and gloom,
> No taper cheer'd the darksome room;
> Yet to the wounded chieftain's sight
> Strange shapes were there, and sheets of light;
> And oft he spoke, in jargon vain,
> Of ruthless deed and tyrant reign,
> For maddening fever fired his brain.
>
> O hark! the warder's rousing call, -
> "Rise, warriors, rise, and man the wall!"
> Starts up the chief, but rack'd with pain,
> And weak, he backward sinks again:
> "O Heaven, they come!" the lady cries,

"The Southrons come and Urquhart dies!"
    Nay, 'tis not fever mocks his sight;
His broider'd couch is red with light;
In light his lady stands confest,
Her hands clasp'd on her heaving breast.
And hark; wild shouts assail the ear,
Loud and more loud, near and more near
They rise!—hark, frequent rings the blade,
On crested helm relentless laid;
Yells, groans, sharp sounds of smitten mail,
And war-cries load the midnight gale;
O hark! like Heaven's own thunder high,
Swells o'er the rest one ceaseless cry,
Racking the dull cold ear of night,
"The Wallace wight!—the Wallace wight!"
    Yes, gleams the sword of Wallace there,
Unused his country's foes to spare;
Roars the red camp like funeral pyre,
One wild, wide, wasteful sea of fire;
Glow red the low-brow'd clouds of night,
The wooded hill is bathed in light,
Gleams wave, and field, and turret height.
Death's vassals dog the spoiler's horde,
Burns in their front the unsparing sword;
The fired camp casts its volumes o'er;
Behind spreads wide a skiffless shore;
Fire, flood, and sword, conspire to slay.
How sad shall rest morn's early ray
On blacken'd strand, and crimson'd main,
On floods of gore, and hills of slain;
But bright its cheering beams shall fall
Where mirth whoops in the Urquharts' Hall.

Edward again marched forces into Moray in 1303 . Sir Alexander Forbes was holding Urquhart Castle for the Scots at that time. Finally after a long, terrible battle did the Scots surrender. The next English constable was Sir Alexander Comyn of Badenoch, who was violently opposed to the new patriot, Robert the Bruce.

Three years later in Scone, that same patriot would be crowned King of Scots. By the summer of 1308, the Bruce had annihilated the Comyns, taken control of the Great Glen and Urquhart Castle. Sir Thomas Randolph, Robert's brave lieutenant, as well as his nephew, was awarded the lordship and the earldom of Moray.

In its heyday the castle housed numerous servants and retainers, in addition to its lord and lady. By the 15th century, the heart of the castle's activity had moved from the upper bailey down to the nether (lower) bailey. Most of the focus was then on the tower-house at its far end. The castle and glens surrounding it were frequently raided and plundered, primarily by the Macdonalds, Lords of the Isles in the 15th and 16th centuries.

For another 150 years Urquhart Castle would be harried and fought over constantly until the grounds and glens were utterly devastated.

Falkirk

The Scottish people were on the verge of starvation, the English having burned homesteads and the livestock having been driven off or killed to feed their army, as well as their grain stolen to feed English destriers. Shortly after Stirling Bridge, Wallace crossed over into England to carry the conflict to its northern territories and to carry home grain and cattle for his people. But as winter advanced, Wallace was forced to return northward toward the end of December. It was during this interval after Wallace's great victory over the English at Stirling that he was knighted, probably by Robert the Bruce, Earl of Carrick.

Wallace realized a great need for more fighting men and much organized training before he could defeat the English again. He had to convert his army into a human fortress and inspire it to withstand a siege. Reminiscent of the ancient Greek phalanx, the schiltron or shieldring was created by Wallace. Each schiltron was a thickly packed circle of spearmen, kneeling or standing with their spears pointing obliquely outwards. He then sent out a general summons to rally men for his army; this request cut across the system of feudal vassalage. Macduff of Fife raised his clansmen and were prepared to do battle, as were men from Galloway, Ayrshire, the North, and the Isles.

By spring of 1298 Wallace's spies informed him that the English were again being mustered for an invasion. Wallace and de Moray's adversaries at Stirling Bridge had grossly underestimated the abilities of the two young patriots. This would not be the case at Falkirk. Edward would be there with his English forces seeking revenge. In preparation Wallace devoted much of his time to drilling the Scots army. Still, it was lacking the skill and power of the great lords.

Edward began his formidable march with disciplined, experienced heavy cavalry north again into Scotland in early July, 1298. Anticipating his advance, Wallace scorched the earth ahead of the English army denying it food for men and horses. For Edward's army, near starvation lay ahead. Wallace continued to lure the English further into barren, hostile country. The Welsh infantry were dying. In response, Edward ordered that wine be given to them to cheer them up. Instead, they became drunk, began a brawl and killed several priests.

July 21st Wallace and his supporters had reached Callendar Wood near Falkirk. He was certain to be able to pursue the retreating English forces barely thirteen miles away. As Edward received this news, he was delighted. "As God lives, they need not pursue me. I will go and meet them this day." Had William a choice, he probably would have sought ground better suited to his advantage, but Edward was eager to do battle. Falkirk would be Wallace's greatest mistake.

Tuesday July 22nd was the day of the feast of St. Mary Magdalene. In her honor at the first rays of morning light, Edward ordered a brief mass for his soldiers before going to slaughter the Scots. The Scottish army was just visible on the hillside, prepared for battle, as the ceremony was completed.

Immediately before the battle, Wallace addressed his troops in the concise manner so characteristic of the man, "I have brought you to the ring. Dance the best you can!"

And that is what they did. The terrifying sight of banners including the Plantagenet leopards, armoured knights astride heavy shire horses pounding down on them, lowered lances, was too much for the smaller Scots cavalry who fled, led by John Comyn the Red. Still, the four schiltrons held fast. Macduff of Fife was killed, leading the men of his earldom. Sir John Stewart, heading his contingent of bowmen, was killed with nearly all his followers.

Historians are yet in debate as to Robert the Bruce's whereabouts. Some place him in the midst of the nobles who deserted Wallace during Falkirk. A few even suggest that he aided Edward. Other chroniclers of the time reason that he wasn't there at all, but at Galloway.

At Falkirk the deadly longbow came into its own. The Welsh archers poured a hail of arrows onto the tenacious Scots. The English cavalry continued to thrust its way into the schiltrons, followed by a large body of English infantry. Falkirk became a hard-fought, long battle with thousands of Scots slaughtered or drowned in the loch nearby.

Records show more than 110 English horses killed on the spears of the schiltrons. Two notable men of rank among the English were lost. Sir Brian le Jay, master of the English Templars, followed Wallace into Callendar Wood and was killed. The master of the Scottish Templars, John of Sawtry also fell at Falkirk.

Despite Edward's victory, he was forced to withdraw his diseased and starving army toward England. Wallace had the foresight to destroy Stirling and its supplies before Edward could reach it. Upon his arrival Edward attempted to repair Stirling Castle and garrison it, knowing full-well its military importance.

The King detoured slightly on his return home, marching through Galloway in search of Bruce. As he reached Ayr on July 26, Edward found that the castle had already been burned by Bruce to prevent the English from benefiting from its shelter and larder. Bruce's beloved Lochmaben Castle suffered from Edward's revenge.

In the days following the battle, William layed low presumably in the thick forests of Scotland. He had made enemies among his own countrymen. His defeat at Falkirk resulted in his loss of a great extent of power in Scotland. As a result of this, he resigned as Guardian. Wallace would have seven more years to live after Falkirk. And even though his army in its present condition was finished, William began a more political fight versus the English.

Tension between France, England, Scotland and the Pope waxed and waned these years like clouds blowing in the tempests' winds.

Pope Boniface VIII constantly used the Scots as a lever to manipulate France and England, both who he feared. The Catholic Church obviously could not be relied upon to intervene in the Scots' cause. Wallace conferred with his ally Bishop Lamberton after Lamberton's return from visiting King Philip of France. Despite Falkirk, William had not lost his constancy of purpose and refusal to compromise. He came to the conclusion that Philip might yet be persuaded to assist the Scottish people.

In August 1299 accompanied by several companions, Wallace set sail for France. Upon Wallace's arrival in Paris, it was obvious that he would be detained while Edward manipulated Philip. Whether coerced or out of boredom isn't certain, but Wallace took 900 men to Guienne in 1300 to fight the English for Philip. Months rolled by until Philip provided William with the proper papers he would need in Rome to beseech the Pope in the Scots' favor.

Having still not lost his passion for action against the English, Wallace traveled on to Rome in the spring 1301. Boniface's greeting was sympathetic at the time. Unfortunately, the Pope again aligned himself with Edward in 1302. William continued to gain support from the Moray family which was closely linked with the Knights Templar and Freemasonry. It was during this trip that he made contact with the Templars. It was the Knights Templar led by a St. Clair, who came to the aid of Wallace's Scottish forces defeating the English at Roslin in 1303. Little else is known of William's activities again until 1303 when he was back in Scotland. But it seems certain that he visited King Haakon in Norway during this period to solicit his support as well.

Wherever Wallace's inspiration was felt, Scotland's spirit of resistance remained. Edward was well-aware of it. To the Hammer of the Scots, Wallace was the last flame of Scottish resistance which had to be extinguished. He accompanied Comyn and Fraser in an armed raid into Annandale and other points south against the English in June, 1303. At Happrew in early 1304, Wallace and his men were defeated by the English. But the English were clearly pounding the Scots into submission, and Wallace was certainly under intense pressure to stay alive.

Edward, in his obsession for revenge on Wallace, offered 100 pounds to the man who could deliver the outlaw to justice. The evening of July 8, 1305 one of Wallace's fellow countrymen Jack Short betrayed him, setting in motion swift events which led to William's capture. It was none other than Sir John Menteith, A Scottish 'nobleman' who handed his country's patriot into Edward's hands.

William Wallace, braveheart that he was, needed all the courage he could muster to endure the seventeen-day journey in scorching summer heat. He rode the entire 300 mile journey with his hands tied behind his back and his feet roped under his horse's belly. William was being parted from his beloved, wild and untamed land. He had seen Scotland for the last time.

August 22 Wallace was presented to the man who had for so many years drenched Scotland in blood. Edward the Plantagenet either would not or could not look in the eyes of the man he was about to condemn to total butchery.

When the dreadful atrocities were completed and Wallace's flesh had fallen away, monks from Cambuskenneth Abby went in the darkness of night to collect the remains of William's left arm. To this day it lies buried at the abbey with its hand outstretched toward Abby Craig.

To Edward, he had defeated an enemy. To the Scottish people, he had created a martyr and rekindled their aspirations, as well as those of Robert the Bruce as their national champion.

A King in Waiting

DeBruce sat astride his heavy charger, watching the Plantagenet with his new 'toy'—a siege engine known as the 'Warwolf'. The Lion Rampant, fast becoming Scotland's royal standard, still fluttered over Stirling Castle's battlements. This engagement had survived Edward's initial attack since May, 1304, but was particularly sickening to see this 20th day of July. The old King's vindictiveness toward the Scottish garrison was blatant, and served to strengthen Robert's resolve.

Barely fifty of the garrison remained alive and were ready to surrender. Yet, the old English warrior was relentless. He ordered the whole power of the siege engines to bombard and batter Stirling's walls. Only after the garrison had fully embarrassed themselves in front of him, did Edward accept their surrender.

Although he could never be sure of de Bruce's loyalties, Edward was certain that he was slowly, methodically winding the Scots totally under his thumb. Once again he misjudged the spirit of the Scots. Survival is a very compelling preoccupation, and Robert had managed for years to play Edward's political game of manipulation. Robert's father had died earlier this same year, passing on to his son the Bruce claim to the Crown of Scotland.

Bishop Lamberton, also determined to rid Scotland of her intruders, conspired with the Bruce on June 11 to once and for all assist each other against Scotland's 'rivals and dangers'. William Lamberton had forever been one of Wallace's staunch supporters. Robert, while never actually supporting him because of the Baliol cause, appreciated Wallace's persistence and determination. When news of the barbaric manner in which William was executed reached the Bruce's ears, there was no longer a shred of doubt where his loyalties lay. Robert the Bruce was no longer content to wait to be King of Scots.

Claiming Celtic heritage through his mother, de Bruce as a young man had gotten off to a doubtful beginning in Scotland's War of Independence. But those qualities of the Celts which make them the best natural material for soldiers on earth, would eventually surface in Robert. The renewal of the revolution in 1306 proved that Bruce would rouse his followers to deeds of valor equal to those of William Wallace.

Comyn the Red, to a degree, involved himself in covert dealings with the King of England. January, 1306 John Comyn agreed with the Bruce to support one another for the Scottish crown. Never to be trusted, Comyn immediately sent word to Edward of the Bruce's idea. Robert, upon his return to the English court, was nearly captured by Edward's men. Fortunately, the King overindulged in wine at supper one evening, revealing his satisfaction to those surrounding him that the Earl of Carrick would soon be out of the way.

A friend passed the information on to Robert immediately, thus allowing him swift passage home. As fortune would have it, Robert encountered another of Comyn's men on the road. The earl's suspicions were alerted. The man was searched, and letters from 'the Red' to Edward were found on him. These papers urgently implored the King to kill Robert.

He had no choice but to force the issue to a solution. On February 10 he met with Red Comyn in Greyfriars Church at Dumfries. The long hostility between the two hot-tempered men came to a head. They quarreled and steel flashed instantly. Forgetting that they stood before the high alter, Robert struck the first blow, sending Comyn sprawling onto the flagstone floor, an act which was to haunt the Bruce for the rest of his life. At this, Robert's companion Kirkpatrick ran into the church and finished Comyn's death. The scene set off a blood-feud with one of the greatest houses in Scotland.

Robert rode hastily to Lochmaben, then on to Bishop Wishart to make confession and to receive absolution. These events signaled an uprising that would raise the Royal Standard and lead the way for Bruce to Scone.

Palm Sunday—March 27, 1306 Robert the Bruce was Crowned King of Scots at the age of thirty-two. The Stone of Destiny having been stolen earlier by Edward, the Chapel Royal of Scone remained the location of the ceremony.

News of John Comyn's murder shocked Edward, causing him to react in his characteristic fury. In April he knighted 250 young noblemen to send into Scotland. Aymer de Valence, Comyn's brother-in-law, was given extensive drastic powers to wield against the new Scottish King whose fortunes were ebbing. Edward next made sure that Bruce's actions at Greyfriars effected his excommunication by the Pope.

Robert's small army met with disaster at the Battle of Methven Wood on June 19th. Here his favorite brother Nigel was captured, then executed. The remaining Scots force headed west and were attacked by the Macdougalls, quite loyal to the Comyn cause. This defeat nearly destroyed Bruce's forces. It was during these days that Robert made two observations: it was 'Celtic Scotland' that supported him, and that he would need to use tactics quite similar to Wallace's guerrilla warfare if he was to be successful in combating the English.

Edward had a firmer grip on Scotland than ever before. King Robert had little choice but to leave the country. On his way in preparation, Robert visited Eilean Donan Castle and his loyal supporters the Macdonalds of Loch Duich there. The time of departure for Ireland then arrived. Midst high winds and winter seas, the Celtic King and his followers of 300 men set sail. Thundering breakers provided an ominous sound to many of the men unaccustomed to sailing. Yet, enough of them were seasoned Hebrideans to make the voyage safely. Quite likely during this voyage, Robert and his sole remaining brother Edward Bruce, gave birth to the idea of uniting a Celtic Confederacy consisting of Scotland and Ireland.

King Robert stayed out of his realm until February, 1307. More and more he was being forced to travel the Highlands and to learn its ways. The Bruce himself was becoming a different person from the earlier feudal nobleman. His concept of Scotland was evolving toward a nation whose people he felt responsibility towards. His experiences of arduous military engagements, political negotiations, private grief, and physical endurance shaped the man into a surer commitment of kingship.

King Edward's health was deteriorating rapidly all this while. Planning yet another invasion into Scotland, the old war-horse collapsed before he could continue his campaign beyond Cumberland. July 7, 1307 he died in sight of the Scottish border.

One afternoon after taking up residence in Ayr, Robert's men spotted the great square sails of impressive sailing vessels headed directly toward their shores. The vivid emblem of the Black Galley of the Isles waved prominently over the lead ship. Angus Og, the Angus, son of Angus son of Ranald, son of Somerled the Great, of Islay, King of the Isles and Lord of Kintyre had come to King Robert's aid! His entire colorful entourage disembarked heralded by the shrill music of blowing pipers; all were garbed in the proud Highland tartans, saffrons, horned helmets, eagles' feathers, piebald calfskins and shining, ornate Celtic jewelry.

Robert, accompanied by another faithful companion, young Jamie Douglas, walked together to the water's edge. The Bruce greeted his longtime friend with open arms. Angus Og smiled openly, "I have come with two-score chieftans, a score of galleys, and a thousand broadswords. Now, together we will see how your enemies fare. I have come to make your war mine!" This single act of comraderie would prove invaluable for many battles and many years to come.

A tenacious band of freedom fighters again rallied behind Bruce at the Pass of Brander in 1308. Angus Og selected a number of his captains, mounted on shaggy Highland garrons, and headed southwest. Robert's only remaining brother Edward took a more 'knightly' assembled force in the opposite direction. This day the Scottish King with the Black Douglas outwitted the Macdougalls in the treacherous mountain pass of Argyll, afterwards capturing Dunstaffnage Castle, the stronghold of that clan.

Eilean Donan Castle on Lock Duich

In a few incredible years, Robert the Bruce had managed to shift the balance of power in Scotland. Both he and his brother Edward had influenced much of Ireland in their favor, as well. The Comyn threat was destroyed, including their allies. March 1309 Robert summoned the first Scottish Parliament at St. Andrews. Philip the Fair even requested the King of Scots to be his ally in a crusade.

Edward II had inherited the English throne but not his father's obsession for conquering the Scottish people. In fact, Edward II would become the Plantagenets' most spectacular failure. A large part of his reign was taken up by self-induced political crisis in England. Nevertheless, he would unwillingly take up a challenge to invade Scotland.

This assembly of forces mustered by Edward was the largest army to ever leave England. Edward meant business and fully expected to conquer Scotland once and for all. He even included a Carmelite versifier in his retinue to sing of his great victory after it was won. His noblemen of the cavalry were especially anxious to do battle, but for a King which they had very little respect for.

Warrior Saints

Crimthann, who later changed his name to Columba, was born in County Donegal, Ireland of a royal family and was raised and educated as a poet. He was learned in pagan, as well as Christian traditions. This background proved useful in later years to overcome his opponents by using his poetic and druidic means. It was the prominent tribe Uí Néill of Ireland that claimed him as a member. Columba had the sacred ability to find and establish the identity of a true king, which was one of the Druids' beliefs in their holy men. Columba was once visited by an angel bearing 'the glass book ordination of kings'. Was it possible that Robert Bruce was one of the choices for future King that Columba saw in this book?

In 563 he left his native country, in penitence for his involvement with warfare, and led a mission to Scotland. With him he carried a vivid scar on his side to remind him of his transgressions. When it served the cause if justice, Columba did not run away form violence. As was common during these times, a penitent was given a sword to be used in settling an unjust score before returning to his former position as a monk. Columba was no different.

He first landed on Jura, later moving to Iona about 569. Eventually, Iona became the most important early Christian monastery in Argyll because of his influence.

Columba soon developed a cult status because of his association with the power as a victory giver. Within fifty years of his death, belief in him was said to guarantee victory in battle. Any relics associated with him were thought to aid in military victory and were considered to be talismans. St. Columba's 'Battler' or 'Cathac,' a prayer book, was carried by the O'Donnells in Ireland to secure their victories. St. Columba filled the descriptions of the earlier pagan, warlike deities. The Gaelic-Norse people of western Scotland considered him as their protector, even comparing him to Odin, the Viking war-god. But Axal was St. Columba's angel and Demal, his devil.

For the Scots preparing to fight near the Bannock Burn, the Monymusk reliquary was the talisman most important to them. This ornate house-shaped box housed St. Columba's relics, and it was hoped would insure the Scots' victory over Edward. June 24, 1314 the Abbot of the monastery at Arbroath carried the reliquary to the site of battle near the Bannock Burn.

Earl Magnus' saga begins in the Orkneys. Descended from the warrior-saint King Olaf of Norway or Saint Ola, Magnus at different times throughout his life said that 'God will shield me. I shall not be killed if He wishes me to live, but I'd rather die than fight an unjust battle'. Instead, Earl Magnus prayed.

During his life there was an attempt by him and his cousin Earl Hakon to share the earldom of Orkney. All went well for many years until malicious people of the community saw fit to create discord by rumor and untruths between them. Eventually, Hakon had his cousin beheaded.

The place of Magnus' death was rocky and overgrown with moss; but as soon as he died, the area became a beautiful meadow. Very soon after Magnus' burial, a dazzling, heavenly light could be seen shining over his grave at night. The people took it for an omen. They began praying to him in times of peril and sickness. Those visiting his grave became aware of a flowery, heavenly fragrance over his grave. Afterward, they would recover their health.

While the population begged for him to be declared a saint, Earl Hakon and Bishop William would not allow it. More and more miracles took place from the gravesite, as well as the relics of Earl Magnus. One day the Bishop himself went blind and sought the grave of Magnus. There he repented and his sight was restored. Twenty years after his death on St. Lucy's Day before Christmas, Magnus was declared a saint.

> The victory of battle standeth not
> in the multitude of a host, but strength
> cometh from heaven.
> They come against us in much pride
> and iniquity to destroy us, and our wives
> and children, and to spoil us.
> But we fight for our lives and our
> laws.
> I Maccabees

Bannock Burn

The day of the fighting at the Bannock Burn must have been the day the angels wept in Heaven to see so many souls marching to their death. The English turned out in a strength of forty thousand, including the cavalry and archers from Ireland and Wales. King Edward II was leading in person with a baggage-train extending for twenty miles behind him. Their advance came by Tweeddale. As the impressive English army neared, their heavy chivalry and longbowmen were sighted. The English had for years specifically bred the strong shire horses to be used in warfare. They could easily be compared to our modern-day tanks. Each animal carried a fully armoured knight in one-hundred pounds of protection and the destrier's armor of five times that weight.

Robert the Bruce's army lay camped in the Torwood. His plan was to use the same tactics as Wallace at Stirling Bridge and Falkirk whereby the Scots would be deployed in schiltrons among the marshy bogs all around the burn.

To further ensure victory, the Bruce had requested the presence of the relics of St. Fillan. These sacred relics of the Celtic Church were entrusted to the care of the Dewars of St. Fillan or monks responsible for the bronze-headed pastoral staff and the Saint's left arm-bone encased in a sliver reliquary. These artifacts, accompanied by that of St. Columba, yielded powerful protection against the English.

As Edward's army reached the area late in the afternoon, he learned of a small corps of Scottish troops near the Carse. Edward ordered an advance of an already mettlesome cavalry regiment. A brazen English knight shouted a challenge to the outstanding Scottish warrior mounted on a small, wiry grey garron. As history records it, Sir Henry de Bohun soon found himself being ridden down by King Robert, accepting the challenge. Despite the fact that de Bohun was well-equipped with a lance, he died instantly as his skull was nearly split in half when the Bruce dealt him a single blow with his battle -axe.

The saints in the heavens were busy at work that night. For early of the morning of June 24th, St. Magnus could be seen valiantly riding throughout the streets of Aberdeen. In his burnished spiritual armour, he rode down out of the clouds on his great white horse and paraded through the city's streets. St. Magnus in his mighty voice declared the Scot's victory at the Bannock Burn, hours before it was over.

The night of the 23rd, the Bruce's troops spent much time in prayer. The Abbot of Inchaffray said mass over the Scottish army. The following day they would face the greatest trial of strength yet put before them.

At sunrise the Scottish footsoldiers were still on their knees in reverence to God. Sir Alexander Seton, one Scottish knight who'd vascillated his loyalties between the English and Scotland, chose this moment to join Bruce. "Now's the time and now's the hour!" declared Seton.

King Robert rose from his bended knee and slowly drew his mighty five foot long, two-handed sword. Raising it high above his head, he dramatically brought it down. "Before God, let us commence!"

The loss for the English was a disaster. Robert had chosen his ground especially well. 'The pows' or slow-running streams wove like spidery webs all through the area. The English cavalry in the lead floundered hopelessly midst the boggy ground and their archers could not find firm footholds to maneuver. Edward had provided no protection for his archery division. From this the Bruce recognized his opportunity and ordered Keith to send his cavalry around to strike the English bowmen.

A gallant five hundred horsemen attacked with a fearsome Scottish war-cry, 'On them! On them!' the same heard fifteen years earlier

Robert the Bruce at Bannock Burn

at Stirling Bridge. The carse ran slippery with blood, mainly English blood. Another banner suddenly appeared midst the Bruce's army, that of the Beausant (the battle flag of the Knights Templar). This proud banner displayed two bars, the upper one black, denoting death to their enemies, the lower one white, denoting peace and love for mankind. Led by their Grand Master Sir William St. Clair (or Sinclair), the skilled warrior horsemen of the Templars had come to the aid of King Robert.

So overwhelming was the Scottish victory that it was taken at the time as an omen that the English would be punished by Heaven for the nation's wrongdoing. The strange, continuous rains which would haunt the English countryside seemed to fulfill this sentiment.

Essentially, Bannockburn won Scotland her freedom, but it did not end the war. Had Edward II the character to admit defeat, thousands more lives in his northern counties would have been saved in years to come.

The October day when Elizabeth and I first visited Bannockburn, we couldn't hear the wild and savage shouting from hundreds, thousands of hoarse throats. Nor did we see or hear the thundering, pounding of hundreds of English shire horses charging to their death upon Scottish spikes of the schiltrons. What was, however, perfectly clear were the sounds of English horn signaling battle and the bagpipes offering courage to Bruce's men.

The Knights Templar

When part of the Templar fleet made its decision to head to Argyll and the Firth of Forth, their Order had been violently dissolved and most of their immense wealth confiscated. Jacques de Molay their last Grand Master had been summarily declared guilty of heinous offenses and burned at the stake by decree of Philip of France. To escape these atrocities, another large fleet of Templars had set sail for the New World and landed on America's New England·coast during the early days of 1308. Considering King Robert's excommunication and continued struggles against England, Scotland was a sanctuary in need of the Knight's warrior skills.

The Knights Templar, originally known as the Poor Knights of the Temple of Solomon, were established in Jerusalem in 1118. Their creation arose from a great need of protection for the Christians during the times of the Great Crusades. With their short hair, long beards, dressed in white mantles with an eight-pointed red cross, off-set on the right shoulder (a Maltese Cross), the original nine Templars were a force which would grow to shape the world. The noble force rode high-spirited Arabian steeds, and their stirrups included much gold. These impressive warriors of Christianity are considered to have been the Guardians of the Holy Grail. What better style to do so than by wielding their gold-guilded, jewel-hilted swords?

From these earliest beginnings, the Sinclair (or St. Clair) family were major influences midst the Templars as Henry Sinclair, the second Baron of Roslin fought in Jerusalem with its new King. Hughes de Payens was the first Grand Master of these men of such devout spirits as monks but the valor of fearsome knights. In 1128 Hughes visited England and Scotland, acquiring great stores of gold and silver in token of gratitude for the Templars' great battles against the Moslems. The numbers of Knights of the Order had grown rapidly to at least five-hundred with numbers constantly fluctuating from fighting losses.

Gradually, the Templars' fame and fortune grew to the point that they were considered the international bankers of the time. Temples were built in their honor, as well as abbeys and cathedrals of great numbers, with these Templars overseeing the work of the masons. Their mission was stated that they wished to 'rebuild Jerusalem' in a manner utilizing elaborate masonry, ornate pillars, and soaring spires.

It is greatly being explored now that the original nine Templars discovered the Nasorean Scrolls of Christ, containing the original teachings of Jesus 'directly to the common people'. These were the concepts of equality, social responsibility and the power of human knowledge. These same Nasorean Scrolls were marked by a star which was called 'Merica' or called by these French knights 'la Merica'. These original knights were startled by their own discovery and were afraid to share it immediately with the rest of the world. Unfortunately, they carried it home to France where total upheaval was only beginning.

Surely Philip the Fair acquired his name from his light complexion, blonde hair and attractive physical features, because it most certainly didn't arrive from any attributes such as principles or scruples. The French King's wars with England had been terribly extensive, resulting in a depletion of the Royal Treasury. Pope Boniface VIII refused to allow the King to tax the Church in order to replenish these funds. However, the Pope was ageing and tired of the continuous bullying and intimidation by Philip the Fair. As the King attempted the Pope's kidnapping and allowed his rough handling, Boniface died shortly thereafter in 1305 as a result.

Benedict XI was his successor and lived only a short while, expiring most likely by poisoning from the direction of King Philip.

The Westford Knight is an image punched into stone of one Templar Knight who landed in la Merica in the 1300's. His shield bears the arms of the Gunn family, related to the Sinclairs. His bascinet type helmet was only used by North Britons between 1350 and 1400.

As the cardinals cowered and delayed in naming Pope Benedict's successor, Philip's envy of the Knights Templars' wealth grew. Within the megalomaniac King of France, a plan to destroy the Order of the Knights was born. And as Pope Clement V was appointed, Philip was convinced he now had a Pope whom he could manipulate to achieve this goal.

It was true that the Order held secret meetings with secret symbols in their ceremonies. These identical symbols and rituals can be found in Freemasonry all over the world today. But the public being omitted from these gatherings began a fantastic series of rumors against the Knights Templar. Tales of devil worshippers and blasphemy were only a few of the falsehoods told against these Crusaders of Christ. These circumstances would serve Philip well in his plans for the Templars, beginning with their unfortunate Grand Master Jacques de Molay.

The King initiated instructions that he wished to merge several similar organizations with that of the Templars. This ploy served to get de Molay and many other of their knights back into Paris. In the meantime, Philip had concocted a list of farfetched accusations against the group. These he filed with the Grand Inquisitor. It was covertly planned that at midnight Friday the 13th of October, 1307 Jacques de Molay and all the Templars in France would be arrested, their archives siezed, and all properties possessed.

As the plan was carried out without a hitch, miraculously a few of the knights quietly learned of Philip's plan, which by now included more of the Pope's participation. The site of what is now Rosslyn Chapel on St. Clair land was where the 'informed' knights congregated in the wake of their demise.

The decision was made for two groups of Templars to venture apart. Consequently, one fleet headed for Scotland. While the second one with the skull and crossbones of the twelve ships' battle flags headed due west on the forty-second parallel. Lord of Rosslyn, Prince Henry Sinclair, also known as the Grand Master of Freemasonry in Scotland, led this mission with three-hundred men to establish a Templar colony, free from suppression.

On a slab of rock in the town of Westford, Massachusetts, there is a carved image of a fourteenth century knight fitting the description of one of the Knights Templar. Carbon dating tests performed on the image shows it to have been drawn in the early 1300's, and is probably the tombstone for one of the Templars who died nearby.

Destinies of the Templars fallen at the ego of King Philip are considered to be the greatest scandal of the Middle Ages. Saturday morning following the imprisonment of de Molay and other Templars, the bewildered Knights were dragged into various courts throughout France, where they were charged with incredible crimes. It was only natural for these honest Crusaders of Christ to exclaim their innocence. Nevertheless through revolting tortures, one-hundred, thirty-eight knights rescinded their vows of innocence. Philip's latest pawn, the new Archbishop of Sens, condemned these as heretics and were sent to the flames to be burned at the stake.

Still, the agony of Jacques de Molay was the last chapter in their murderous saga. The aged Grand Master would further be betrayed by the Roman Catholic Church and its Pope whom they'd served so loyally. De Molay was dragged in heavy chains from his dungeon beneath the Paris Temple. Some assume that he was then burned in slow fires of charcoal and fagots. Others now are certain that he was crucified, flayed with horse whips with metal balls, and then had a crown of thorns placed on his head. Hours after his horrible ordeal, Jacques de Molay was wrapped in his own 'Masonic' shroud, quite possibly the one known today as the Shroud of Turin.

In 1988, Scientists concluded after testing scraps of the 14 foot long, 3 1/2 foot-wide linen that is dated back to between 1260 and 1390. Not only do these dates concur with the death of de Molay, but the face imprinted on the Shroud of Turin matches that of the aged Grand Master.

The white-haired Grand Master issued a pardon, as well as a warning to Philip, as his last dying words. "In Heaven there is an august tribunal to which the weak never appeal in vain. To that tribunal I summon the Roman pontiff within 40 days. Philip, I pardon thee in vain, for thy life is condemned. At the tribunal of God, within a year, I await thee."

As history moved on, this edict apparently issued the beginning of the Hundred Years War. What was immediate, however, was that Pope Clement died of dysentery within a year. King Philip also answered the summons issued from the flames only months following the death of the Pope.

Rosslyn Chapel

In the town of Roslin slightly south of Edinburgh, there stands a magnificent structure designed and built by William Sinclair. Rosslyn Chapel took forty-five years to complete and is a testimony to the Knights Templars' journeys to and from America. The aloe cactus and Indian maize carvings adorn the pillars of this ediface, plants which were indigenous to America at the time and supposedly 'undiscovered' until Christopher Columbus' voyage in 1492.

Rosslyn Chapel, with its giant buttresses and elaborate pinnacles, measures 35 feet by 69 feet with a roof height of 44 feet. Ground for the structure was first broken in 1441. Then by 1486 the hundreds of stone carvings adorning its walls and ceilings, telling tales of the Bible, were in place and work was completed. Angels and masonic figures also decorate the inside.

Sensitive visitors to Rosslyn Chapel today are aware of the spiritual presence of the boy who carved the famous 'Prentice Pillar'. At the spot beside the beautiful work he accomplished, the illuminated essence of the murdered youth can still be found weeping hundreds of years after his death. The Master Mason had returned from a long journey and found that the apprentice's work was being lauded over the land. In his jealousy the primary mason stabbed the boy to death, whereupon a curse fell on his own life.

Moira Robertson

The Boaz Pillar or 'Apprentice Pillar' designed by the ill-fated apprentice. Interior of Rosslyn Chapel depicting maize and aloe plants from 'la Merica.'

Moira Robertson

The western end and entrance to Rosslyn Chapel.

A side view of Rosslyn Chapel with its flying buttresses and ornate spires.

The Last Crusade

After their aid at Bannockburn, King Robert rewarded the Knights Templar with a bishopric and additional lands. He also recognized the continued danger to the Templars and ordered that they become a secret organization. Thus the Royal Order of Scotland was established to reward their courage at Bannockburn.

So many events were going wrong in England as of 1315. The lashing downpours drove her people into despair. The English crops rotted in the fields, flooding covered the countryside, famine and disease were rampant. At the same time King Robert sent his raiders into English territory, forcing citizens to buy them off.

The name of the Black Douglas sent terror through the hearts of northern England. If Edward I had been the Hammer of the Scots, Jamie Douglas was his counterpart, earning the name of Hammerer of the English. Jamie had joined Robert's forces at a young age. Through the years he'd become one of Bruce's most courageous followers. The Black Douglas was now determined to exact a great vengeance for the wrongs he, his father, and Scotland had suffered.

The Bruces had held for sometime the idea of uniting Ireland and Scotland in a Celtic Confederacy. When the O'Neills invited Edward Bruce into Ireland to be their King, the possibility of this union became even stronger. Besides, Scotland was becoming too small for the two brothers.

Fifteen years separated Bannockburn from Robert the Bruce's death. His consistent objective through these years was to win recognition from England of his own position in Scotland, as well as full renunciation of the English Crown's claims to suzerainty over Scotland. This was difficult enough without some of his subjects continuing to give him trouble.

On the bleak moors of southern Scotland quite close to the English border, lies what remains of the estate of William de Soulis. During these days of continued unrest, de Soulis unsuccessfully launched a plot to seize the crown from King Robert. One version of history indicates that de Soulis was consigned to prison where he died. However, local Border inhabitants recall another, more sinister version of the activities surrounding Hermitage Castle and its lord, William de Soulis.

Black magic was William's passion, taking him to the studies of a master wizard. He quickly became one of the wizard's most adept students. In the dungeons of Hermitage Castle, de Soulis murdered kidnapped children and used their blood to summon ghoulish monsters. His passion grew far out of control as he roamed the countryside frequently in search of young victims.

The people of the community cried repeatedly to King Bruce for aid. Finally, he responded, unaware that they would take his word so literally. De Soulis was captured, wrapped in a sheet of lead, and boiled in a cauldron.

To this day midst the menacing sandstone ruins of the castle, William's spirit is heard with that of his victims in bone-chilling screams and devilish laughter.

Robert the Bruce's health failed him more rapidly. What he considered to be his curse brought upon himself by killing Comyn the Red, was called leprosy. This crippling illness would gradually take his last breath on June 7, 1329. Until that time though, Robert made trips into Ireland to ensure positive relations there. He fervently continued to pay homage to St. Fillan, the most renowned Scoto-Irish saint.

After the Declaration of Arbroath in 1320, the Scots' response to the excommunication of the Bruce, Jamie Douglas, and the Earl of Moray, the people of Scotland made more headway. Then as the Treaty of Edinburgh was agreed upon in 1328, peace temporarily lay around Scotland. They had won everything that they had fought for. Her population was near starvation and her economy was in shambles. But Scotland had won her freedom from England and the complete acknowledgment of her right to it. Robert the Bruce knew Scotland and her people as no King before him or since has done. He'd asked of Scotland a miracle and she'd accomplished it.

It had always been Robert's wish to fight the 'Saracens' in the Holy Land, to journey on a crusade. His last dying wish was that his heart should be removed from his body, embalmed, and carried into battle against God's enemies. To the brave and faithful Sir James Douglas, the honor fell.

Wearing the Bruce's heart in a tiny casket of silver about his neck, the Black Douglas, Sir William Sinclair, and a lively contingent of Scotland's knights went into battle on March 25, 1330 in Andalusia. The Moorish cavalry were superior to their forces, particularly after a feint attack. So many of the famous knights died in the foray—the Logans, William Sinclair, including Jamie himself.

William Keith personally brought back the remains of Sir Douglas and the courageous heart of Robert the Bruce, finally getting to make that last crusade. Today that courageous heart lies in its miniature casket at Melrose Abbey in the Borders.

The Highlanders

The clan in its original Celtic form was a patriarchal, organized society. Clansmen fought for and provided for their chief and his family as representatives of all their ancestors. Laws of succession, inheritance and land tenure were firmly established and rarely questioned. Essentially, for several centuries following the Bruce's death, life among the clans particularly in the Highlands would continue much as it had before Bannockburn. Yet in those years immediately following 1314, the Highland clans truly came into their own individual character, development and power.

Chief Neil led his men of Clan Campbell at Bannockburn. To further his alliance with the Bruce, he married Robert's sister Mary. Lochaweside became their main position of strength. As they were awarded extensive lands previously owned by the MacDougalls, enemies of King Robert, the Star of the Campbells of Argyll was on the rise. They would soon grow to become a force to be reckoned with.

Angus Og MacDonald of Islay became Clan Chief and was very powerfully rewarded for his support of Robert the Bruce. Angus was awarded Morvern, Ardnamurchan, the islands of Mull, Coll, Tiree and part of Lochaber.

Long the allies of Clan Donald, Clan Gilleans or the MacLeans, also fought at Bannockburn led by Chief Malcolm. The 'Spartans of the North' as they were called, were quite the formidable sea-power, holding fort at the mighty stronghold of Duart Castle. They too benefited greatly from King Bruce's rewards.

Clan Cameron is believed to have developed from vassals of the MacDonalds and possibly also from the MacDuffs the premier clan of Gaels. Lochaber was the Cameron foothold. By 1345 intense clan warfare had begun with their neighbors the MacKintoches, backed by Clan Chatten, against the Camerons. This battling back and forth would prove to extend into the next three hundred years.

In the early 1400's Black Donald, then the Cameron Chief, was recognized as a great warrior. The famous 'pibroch' of this group served as a march for the Queen's Own Cameron Highlanders, as well as the clan itself. The family continued to grow and establish itself as one of great military tradition.

Sir Ewen Cameron would prove to be the last Highland chief to hold out for Charles II against Cromwell. Then in 1793 Allan Cameron raised the 79th Regiment which in 1881 became the Queen's Own Cameron Highlanders. On the soils of America of 1858, a militia unit would be formed from the Scottish immigrants, veterans of the Crimean War, evicted to make room for sheep. Thus the 79th New York Highlanders was born.

The Misty Isle of Skye is one of great scenic beauty. Landscape with the jagged ridges of the Black Cuillins Mountains dominating the scene is breathtaking. Visitors of today circuiting the coastline may even spot a Golden Eagle. But what is even more curious a spectacle is that of 'the Silent Ones,' a ghostly squadron of fifty Highland soldiers tramping menacingly along Skye's roads. Complete with 'claidheamh mor,' basket-hilted broadswords, cowhide targes, and lochaber axes, the completely soundless troops are spotted many times during the year.

Several of the local people on Skye who have witnessed this phenomenon say that 'the Silent Ones' are either MacDonalds or MacLeods who were frequently at odds for centuries.

The MacLeods claim their Viking ancestry from Olaf the Black. From him indirectly they acquired lands on the Isles of Skye and Harris and North Uist. In time the MacLeods of Dunvegan became the clan chiefs. Their earliest loyalties lay with the Lords of the Isles. More and more the MacLeods of Dunvegan rose to strength.

In 1480 the MacDonalds raided Skye claiming MacLeod lands. So that by 1528 the bloody battle of Glendale erupted where the unfurling of the MacLeod's Fairy Flag saved the day.

The 8th Chief, Alastair established a MacCrimmon piping school on Skye which grew to fame. As the bagpipes are not original to the Scottish Highlands but are found in many lands, it was to Alastair's credit that he was so 'instrumental' in their growth of popularity. The bagpipes were not introduced to Scotland until the 14th century. The pipes quickly became a powerful tool of warfare as they invoked acts of heroism.

The 'clarsach' or ancient Celtic harp of the Highlands, long used by the bards who sang of the chiefs' achievements and of the clans' histories, was the national instrument of Scotland. Chief Alastair's school of MacCrimmon pipers altered that so that the bagpipes then assumed that honor.

A later chief Rory 'Mor' continued the support of the bards, harpers and pipers. In 1596 Rory 'Mor' also campaigned in Ireland with the O'Neills against Queen Elizabeth I. One sept of these Irish O'Neills settled on Harris Island as bards after Rory 'Mor' MacLeod's return to Dunvegan. It was this group of O'Neills who assumed the name Morrison.

The magnificent Castle of Dunvegan is in excellent condition, particularly attributable to such additions as the Fairy Tower during Chief Alastair's lifetime. Today it's home to the legendary Fairy Flag of the MacLeods. Other relics to be found on display are the sword of Major Donald MacLeod of St. Kilda who fell leading the charge of the Royal Highland Emigrant Regiment at Moore's Creek, North Carolina in 1777 in the American Revolutionary War. A mid-eighteenth century regulation dirk of the 42nd Regiment, known as the Black Watch, was also recovered form the battlefield at Moore's Creek and is on display at the castle. It is notable that the Highland Emigrant Regiment were granted the right to wear the 'Black Watch' accoutrements in America.

Most of Clan Morrison is also believed to be descended from Olaf the Black of Viking history. Olaf's son was shipwrecked on the coast of Lewis Island and washed ashore. It was he who was the progenitor of this aspect of Clan Morrison.

The Morrison Clan chiefs of Lewis became the hereditary brieves of that island. According to genealogists, these chiefs are also descended from a cadet of Clan Donald and are in direct male line from Somerled the Great, King of the Isles, slain in 1164.

Intermingling and intermarriages between the MacLeods and Morrisons gradually led to disagreements. Then the MacKenzies eventually claimed the Isle of Lewis through marriage, and war ensued with the Morrisons siding with the MacKenzies.

It is no small wonder that the story of Shannon Morrison took the bend that it did. Shannon was born near Stowe, Vermont in 1990. At the age of two , she became especially attentive to only one song played on an old 78 rpm record that her parents owned. That single piece of music was the only one with bagpipes in it.

Shannon sat on the floor transfixed, staring at the antiquated record player. The child knew little words, but she managed to sputter out, "horsies, Mommie, horsies," while big 'crocodile tears' poured down her cheeks.

Her parents were mystified. If left alone with the music, Shannon would cry until she was nearly inconsolable. Her parents finally had to hide the record. Even then the child would find it and manage to put it on to play, leading to the inevitable tears and talk of "horsies".

As Shannon aged two more years, her parents were hopeful that she'd have forgotten about her attraction to the bagpipes. However while thumbing through a magazine one evening, Shannon spotted a colorful Highlander playing his pipes. The child recognized them immediately. "Daddy, look! Look at the bagpipes. I want to learn how to play them," she announced.

'Wherever in the Green Mountains of Vermont in 1994 were they going to find someone to teach their daughter how to play the pipes?' her parents wondered, not seriously considering the idea.

For the next year, the girl collected pictures and any scraps of information on bagpipes. Meanwhile, her parents still hoped it was a 'passing phase'.

When Ian MacLeod and his wife left Scotland the spring of 1995 to visit friends in America, he absently found himself packing his bagpipes. His wife watched him carefully wrap them in their case before asking, "Why are you packing those, Ian?" Her husband only traveled with them for ceremonies or competitions.

He searched for the answer, "I don't really know. But I feel like there is a reason to do so". So Ian MacLeod arrived in Stowe, Vermont with his bagpipes April, 1995. Within two days of their arrival, the MacLeods went cross-country skiing. Ian, dressed in warm clothing, still was a bit noticeable sporting his beautiful plaids of his tartan trews and stockings.

Shannon and the Morrison family had also chosen that day for an outing on ski's. Shannon spotted the MacLeods immediately and gravitated to Ian like a magnet. The young girl unabashedly questioned him about bagpipes. The Scotsman grinned from ear to ear. "Yes," he proudly announced, "I happen to have brought them on the trip."

Arrangements were made eventually for the child to take lessons from Ian. Everyday for the next two weeks, Shannon faithfully learned to play the bagpipes. Now three years since, she is competitively one of the finest youth pipers in the United States.

I visited Dunvegan Castle in May, 1997. I particularly navigated toward one outstanding portrait in the grand dining room. It was the melancholy painting of one of the MacLeod's Ladies who'd died centuries ago. I found myself staring at the face of Shannon Morrison, my cousin.

As of 1377 extensive Celtic inheritances were falling into Anglo-Norman possessions. The old Celtic earldoms were disappearing as new clans were being formed. The Gordons, Frasers, Grants, Hays and Innesses were but a few which sprung up, headed by chiefs of Anglo-Norman origin.

The clans during the sixteenth century had reached the height of their aggressions toward each other, playing politics with the Crown to vie for power. One example was Campbell of Ardkinglas who made sure that the MacGregors were nearly exterminated. The men, including their Chief Alastair, were executed in Edinburgh while the women and children were transported to Ireland.

The connection between the Scottish Highlands and Ireland had been close for many centuries. As the English had adverse effects on Ireland, its customs and dress as they were forced to abandon their distinctive dress, it had considerable repercussions on the Scottish Highlander kinfolk. After all, the Scots were originally an Irish tribe who much earlier had given their name to ancient Alban. It is no wonder that in the New World of America, the two societies would have perfect opportunity to unite in freedom.

As the Crowns gained more power and politics were allowed to play a highly active role in manipulating citizens' lives, the fortunes of the clans declined to their ultimate ruin—the downfall of the old patriarchal sense of the clan. They would be destroyed on Drumossie Moor (Culloden), whereafter they would be hunted down, robbed, outraged, and massacred.

Worchester, 1651

Through the early 17th Century, Scotland was in the throes of religious controversy. Charles I, crowned King in 1633, was convinced that it was his duty to the citizens of Scotland to bring them back under the wing of the Church of England. Most of Charles' reign was spent installing strict changes in this direction. By February, 1638 an impressive gathering of representatives and noblemen met in Edinburgh to sign a National Covenant to protect thier "true religion."

The Covenanters also firmly believed that they were protecting their country from becoming an English province. Consequently, the movement to uphold strong Presbyterian beliefs was as much political as it was religious.

Autumn of 1641 the political situation in England was coming to a head and Charles sought support from Scotland for his disputes with Parliament. The Scottish populace remained separate from the situation when English civil war erupted between Parliament and their King's supporters. Under the formidable leadership of Oliver Cromwell, the Parliamentary forces were growing in strength.

The Earl of Montrose who was one of the organizers of the committee signing the National Covenant was experiencing a change of heart (or politics). In 1644 Montrose rode northward into Scotland to establish a small Scottish army in support of the King. As the Lowlanders were firmly backing the Covenanters, Montrose turned to the Highlanders. Through covert travels, secret meetings, and calling on trusted friends, the brilliant Montrose soon raised the flag for the Royal cause. Among the ready volunteers were the MacLeans whose Chief Lachlan was made a baronet of Nova Scotia by King Charles. Alasdair MacColla MacDonald commanded over a thousand Irish levies sent by the Earl of Antrim. Even more MacDonalds took the role of Cavaliers, many of which were from the Glen Coe region. Still other clans who had old scores to settle against the Covenanting Campbells, were eager to follow the Marquis of Montrose in the Scottish Wars of the Covenant (also known as the Civil War).

Montrose's Highland fighters were masters as usual, winning battles at Dundee, Auldearn, Kilsyth, and more. Yet, the Covenanters would not be converted. Over time some troops deserted, some defected, and many were killed. Montrose slowly watched his small army dissipate.

May, 1646 King Charles surrendered and the Marquis of Montrose was left to disband his remaining Highland forces. Within three years King Charles was executed in Whitehall.

Following his father's death, Charles II assumed the throne, but stayed safely in exile until 1650. With the aid of a Scottish army of Highlanders, Charles II decided to win back his father's throne. Montrose had been betrayed by one of his old acquaintances and had been hanged. So, Charles was left to his own devices to raise an army. The Glen Coe MacDonalds again rose to the occasion, as did the MacLeans. Although formerly opposed to Montrose, the Frasers, Campbells, MacLeods, and MacKenzies now gathered to support the Royal Standard.

Oliver Cromwell at age fifty-two was still the powerful general of the Parliamentary army and was a disrupting threat in the Scottish countryside. As thier reputation proves, the Highlanders (especially the MacLeans) stood and fought while the Lowlanders fled from the English attack. After Inverkeithing in the spring of 1651, Cromwell lured Charles into a trap, so that marching into English territory was inevitable.

Charles hoped to acquire further support from Wales, thus taking his men toward Worchester. But forces under Generals Lambert and Harrison, as well as Cromwell's from the north were racing to prevent this. Poorly supplied and exhausted, the Scottish army entered Worchester on August 22, 1651. Charles was to receive no aid from the local citizens who only saw them as an invading force.

Meanwhile, Oliver Cromwell carefully planed his attack. Then on September 3 his men advanced over an eight-mile front around Worchester, with a reserve held by Cromwell himself on higher ground. As the Royalists were not anticipating an attack this day, Cromwell was at an advantage. After watching the fighting begin, from his location atop Cathedral Tower, King Charles descended to join the battle, offering inspiration to his men.

Fierce hand-to-hand combat led on. The intervention of Parliamentary reserve troops took the Highlanders by surprise. Still the Scots stood against the enemy, however hopeless it seemed. The Parliamentary fire-power was more impressive than the Highlanders'. Scottish bodies littered the streets. The battling extended long into the afternoon before the gates of Worchester were taken. The surviving Highlanders retreated as cannon full of grape-shot were fired upon them. Numerous tenacious Scots remained fighting from house to house, whereby Cromwell's men saw fit to round up and chase stragglers.

Some 3,000 Highlanders retreated from Worchester only to be ambushed by their adversaries. King Charles eluded capture and went into hiding for several weeks. Oliver was left to be master of both England and Scotland. The fate of 10,000 prisoners had yet to be decided.

The death sentence was determined for many. A high percentage of the mettlesome Highlanders would never see home again. These were sent to Ireland, serving a military sentence there. Another large group of prisoners were shipped to the New World and dispersed into the slave colonies for work on tobacco and sugar plantations. These locations included Virginia, the West Indies, with others sailing to New England.

The Battle of Worchester, 1651 is re-enacted every two years at the Museum of American Frontier Culture in Staunton, Virginia. September 6 and 7, 1997 Captain Jaymes (Dale) Shinn and his Fellow Patriots in the Service of the most Excellent Marquis of Montrose arrived from Sacramento, California. Shinnes' Free Artillery Companie, as well as re-enactors from Scotland and England, would recreate the battle.

Shinns (Sheen) were originally from the Sudentenland, the furthermost northeastern territory of Scotland. Today, a ruined castle still stands on Loch Shin. John and his wife Jane emigrated to New Jersey in 1678, from where Capt. Jaymes' family branch moved to North Carolina, then to Arkansas in 1832.

Dale comes by his talents and loyalties to the Scottish Highlanders honestly. His father passed on exciting tales of wanderings in the woods with various firearms. Spurred by that interest and his own collecting, he committed 25 years ago to enter the realm of gunsmithing and to capture a by gone era. Early on he struggled to learn how to recreate authentic weapons from the 16th and 17th centuries.

As fate would have it, Dale came face-to-face with one of his relatives from centuries ago. One night through the haze of a dreamy night, he met that most famous of early Gunsmiths, Bartholomew Marquart of Augsburg, a mechanical genius who King Charles V of Spain, took to Madrid to fashion weapons for him. No words were spoken between them, but Dale awoke with a renewed sense of approval and connection.

The Swedish Leather Cannon has long been of special interest to Capt. Shinn. It is a lightweight fabricated piece of copper and steel with canvas and leather shrunk over it. In his gunner's able hands Gustavus Adolphus, effectively changed the tactics and face of warfare in the 1600's. Later Robert Scott in Gustavus' service returned to Scotland and bought his version of the "Leathern cannon" to the face of the English Civil War battlefield.

Roland Selis, one of the crew, discovered a published monogram on the only extant Leather cannon in Sweden. The treatise provided Dale with the necessary details to fashion the leather cannon used at the re-enactment of the Battle of Worchester. Eric Erricson, another crew member talented in stage crafts, helped finish the barrel and shrink the canvas and leather over it. Gene Morrow, a cannoneer of many decades, created the cannon tools and contributed many insights and suggestions.

Above: Cromwell's men driving back the Highlanders toward Worchester.

Right: Dale Shinn, Captain of the Leather Guns—playing the hurdy gurdy.

Captain Jaymes Shinnes Free Artillery Companie in the service of the Army of the Marquis of Montrose, pictured with the leather cannon.

Washington and the Son's of Erin

Rumor of the times said that Cromwell had sold his soul to the devil as payment for his victory at Worchester. He was to die on the exact anniversary of that battle seven years afterward. Unfortunately, before that passing, Oliver Cromwell exacted a merciless ravage on Ireland. Thousands of Irish citizens joined their fellow Celts of Scotland who were exiled as slaves or indentured servants. As so many were sent to the West Indies, a number of them were fortunate to escape and find their way to America.

Through song, the Irish cast their lots as wanderers. History would prove later that they could redeem themselves. Early in the North American settlements, the Irish proved to be fierce fighters against Indians.

Virginia and the Carolinas' coastline received the Irish immigrants from the Barbados in 1678. In the early 1700's the Blue Ridge Mountains were settled by another Irish contingency. Augusta County, Virginia became the residence in 1736 of yet another group of Irish established by James Patton. Patton's determination to reestablish his Celtic friends became evident when he crossed the sea 25 times, returning with boat loads of Irish families. Andrew Meade from County Kerry in Ireland settled in Virginia late in the 17th century. General George Meade, Commanding General of the Army of the Potomac, so victorious at the Battle of Gettysburg, was a descendant of Andrew Meade.

George Washington's family was closely intertwined with Irish immigrants since 1691. The McCarthy family, also neighbors from Ireland, became very close friends with the Washingtons. George, early in his life and continuing through his entire life, maintained a close relationship with the Irish community. As his years advanced, as well as his ambitions to solidify America into unity, George Washington's practice as a Freemason became even stronger. He closely allied himself with countless other Freemasons who founded our great country.

The notions of independence and liberty for all mankind had come from distances across many seas. It would not be long before the new emigrants, both Scottish and Irish, would find themselves in the midst of the American Revolution where they would be pitted against relatives and others of their own countrymen. At the formation of our Continental Army, four-fifths of General Washington's forces were of Irish descent or Irish-born. The "Line to Ireland" was the famous Pennsylvania Line led by General Light-Horse Harry Lee.

Upon Washington's retreat to Valley Forge in 1777, he was visited by an angelic inspirational force who addressed him as the "Son of the Republic". During this divine visitation, Washington was shown visions of America as the greatest Union of men on the planet. He was reminded repeatedly to "Remember ye are brethren," and that "While the stars remain, and the heavens send down dew upon the earth, so long shall the Union last". That final campaign in 1781 at Yorktown was victoriously influenced by a high count of Irish blood.

By 1782 Washington had been made Honorary member of the Sons of St. Patrick. In accepting the honor he wrote, "With great pleasure I accept the ensign of such a fraternity, that society distinguished for the firm adherence of its members to the glorious cause in which we are embarked".

"Observe good faith and justice towards all nations; cultivate peace and harmony with all. Religion and morality enjoin this conduct.... It will be worthy of a free, enlightened....great nation, to give mankind the magnanimous ... example of a people always guided by an exalted justice and benevolence," words quoted from George

Washington's farewell address are undeniably similar to those among the creeds of the Freemasons, as well as the teachings of Jesus Christ, guarded so fervently by the Knights Templar.

Warrior Poets

Glen Coe, with its air of mystery, can be a wild and tempestuous place, steeped in history. In the spring her winds are warm, the red deer moving gracefully on the braes below the fading snowline. Summer sees days of sun and color, when grey - leg geese wing lazily across the loch. The mountain peaks at dusk have a special etherial quality. How peaceful it can seem.

The most historical figure connected with Glen Coe was St. Mundus, an Irish disciple of St. Columba who came from Iona about 600 A.D. St. Mundus settled briefly on a small island in Loch Leven. Thus it was named Eilean Munde, becoming the religious center of the region.

The glen has an abundance of lore regarding witches and giants. The wicked Corrage was its most famous witch, who was surprisingly offered burial on Eilean Munde. The citizens of Loch Leven rebelled at the idea, however, and prevented it from happening. Befitting the size of Glen Coe's mountains, cloud-veiled rock faces and deep gullies, she was also once the home of Fingal (or Fionn) a great Celtic hero. Fionn MacCumhail was the leader of the Feinn, warriors of Gaelic mythology. Fionn, who lived long before St. Mundus, is credited in folk ballads and poems with the defeat of the Vikings in the glen.

Named after him are Sgor nam Fiannaidh (the rock of the Feinn) and Fionn Ghleann (Bright Glen). The cave high above Loch Achtriochtan is named after Ossian, Fingal's poet son.

From about the 11th century until 1308, Glen Coe belonged to the powerful MacDougall clan, of Viking descent, whose base was Dunstaffnage Castle near Oban. As the MacDougalls sided in favor of John Balliol and the English against Robert the Bruce in 1308, their power was shattered. Ironically, the MacDonalds and Campbells fought side-by-side for Bruce in the destruction of the MacDougalls at the Battle of the Pass of Brander, south of the glen. Angus Og, Chief of the MacDonalds, was rewarded with the area by the Bruce. For the following five-hundred years, it remained MacDonald country.

Trouble began in the glen about the year 1500. The MacDonalds of Glen Coe and the nearby MacGregors tended to augment their livings by cattle-rustlings to their south. The more prosperous clan Campbell were becoming more and more ambitious in extending their lands. This basic conflict went on for three-hundred years.

Black Colin, first Laird of the Campbell clan, inherited Glen Orchy from his father. This narrow, twisting valley runs south-westward from Rannoch Moor to Loch Awe. The great Castle Kilchurn was built by Black Colin from the ruins of a MacGregor keep. From this magnificent stronghold, the Campbells conducted their merciless feud against the MacGregors to rid them, not only from this land, but from total extinction. All those who succeeded him also did what they could to fulfill Black Colin's ambition by acquiring more land holdings from various clans.

Gradually, the Campbells gained backing of the government's support in Edinburgh. By marriage, force and trickery, the Campbells took over lands of their less fortunate neighbors. The encounters between the MacDonalds and Campbells went on for years leading up to that fateful night in 1692.

The MacDonalds claimed the lands of the Hebridean Isles from the Butt of Lewis to South Uist, from Skye to Jura and Islay. They claimed Lochaber, Ardnamurchan and Kintyre. In Ireland they filled the glens of Antrim. No matter what history bestowed upon them, the MacDonalds believed themselves to be the lords of Gaeldom.

Alastair, 12th Chief of the MacDonalds of Glen Coe, was a violent man, as well as a thief, yet dignified and intensely loyal to the family tradition and his own code. This loyalty included the Highland code. Safety and happiness of MacIain came before all. He was Clan Iain

Abrach; as he prospered, none else in the clan would want. His clansmen concluded each meal with grace in which the Almighty God was asked to give attention to his welfare and protection. "May your chief have the ascendancy!" said a Highlander, wishing another good fortune.

Highlanders, particularly the MacDonalds themselves, believed that all men of Glencoe were poets from birth. The spirit of man is instinctively poetic, seeking expression in imagery. Only an age of people which has abdicated its emotions to professionals has forgotten this and lost touch with their true Souls. For all the savagery and sweetness of the life of the warrior poets of Glencoe, they sought an immortality in verse. Yet, most of it died when their voices were stilled in that darkness of February 13, 1692.

The story of the Massacre at Glen Coe is one of tragedy between two conflicting ways of life, the old and the new—the carefree, ebullient Highland reivers and the ruthless, sober central government. August, 1691 King William III offered pardon to all Highland clans who had fought against him or raided their neighbors, in exchange for oath of allegiance before an official magistrate before January 1, 1692.

October scattered the clansmen; there were more storms on the loches and flurries of snow on the high braes. November, the weather was cruel enough already. To breathe deeply was to feel a knife in the lungs. December began with great storms and squalls of snow, emphasizing the black hostility of the mountains.

The old warrior chief MacDonald delayed until the last few days. December 30th he struck out, finally determined to sign the agreement. Alastair was deterred by Government troops and delayed by bad weather, causing him to arrive two days late. He was then kept waiting three more days, taking the oath five days late.

Unfortunately, forces of the government had already been set in motion against the Glen Coe MacDonalds. King William, John Campbell (the Earl of Breadalbane) and Sir John Dalrymple of Stair (the Secretary of State) all believed that the clan deserved no mercy.

Dalrymple's power and determination to crush the Highlanders was obsessive. Much of his character and success was attributed to the supernatural practices of the black arts which his family was active in. Witchcraft and black violence were believed to be inseparable from the Dalrymples. "Be earnest, be Secret and Sudden, be quick," was the edict sent by Sir John Dalrymple.

On February 1, advance companies of Government troops were sent to Glen Coe under the command of Captain Robert Campbell of Glen Lyon, whose niece happened to be married to the chief's younger son. Captain Campbell requested quarters for his two companies in the homes of the Glen Coe folk. For ten days all were warmly entertained and provided for.

The Celts of the glen were not aware of the strange and terrible warnings that had been evident to others, 'An Duine Mor,' the Great Man who appeared only when gentlefolk are in danger, was seen by the loch at Ballachulish on Friday . That same afternoon, some of the cows at Carnoch broke from the byre and ran up the brae, crying pitifully, yet nothing was seen to startle them.

For several days in advance, the 'Bean Nighe' had been seen by the waterfalls of the Coe, a supernatural washing-woman who cleansed a shroud again and again, but none who saw her had the courage to ask whose it might be.

For many nights the 'Caoineag,' the keening woman who could be neither approached nor addressed, but who always foretold death, had been heard.

The night of the 12th was bitter cold, the wind even stronger as the snow thickened. Orders from Glenlyon were given in the darkness and the wind, lest the news be received by the victims' ears. Campbell and his men were to kill all MacDonalds under 70 years of age the following morning.

A great fire would be lit at 5:00 a.m. on Signal Rock, so that the red coats would know when to begin the slaughter which would take place in several parts of the glen.

This was to be the ultimate breach of the ethic of Highland hospitality. 120 Government men were ordered to destroy, in poor weather and darkness, several hundred people in their sleep, including Campbell's own niece and husband. Among these troops, a dozen were Campbells.

Before dawn, John MacDonald was awakened by voices outside his house. As he went to the window, he saw flames of pine-knots, red coats and dark bonnets, the barrels of muskets shining in the firelight. He trekked through hurling wind to Inverrigan's house which Glenlyon was using as temporary headquarters. Once inside, John was assured by the Campbells that they'd only received orders to move against Glengarry's men. The MacDonald was content with this explanation. He grasped Glenlyon's hand, wished him well on his march, then returned home to sleep.

The first to be killed was Duncan Rankin who lived near the chief's house. He was shot from behind while running from the soldiers toward the river. Lieutenant Lindsay's men marched next to MacIain's house at Carnoch. There they entered and shot the elderly chief twice in the back, as they yelled the vengeful cry of Clan Campbell. MacIain's wife's clothes were ripped from her body and the rings torn off her fingers.

At Achnacon several people were killed, an old man of eighty and a child. Then at Achtriochtan where the clan bards lived, another group was murdered. Midst their ruthlessness, general incompetence saved the lives of many potential victims. About thirty-eight MacDonlads died while three-hundred or so escaped. In the days ensuing the massacre, many died of starvation and cold.

For long moments, one could hear shots and cries, then nothing but the sound of the keening wind. As the snow swirled and parted, one could see the glow of flames from the burning homes. By afternoon of that day, a Saturday, there lingered the smell of death, and the trampled snow was red with MacDonald blood.

Whether the lyrics came from the Jacobites or poets such as Murdoch Matheson who survived the massacre, sentimental ballads would long be cried in the streets of Edinburgh.

> "On that dark and fateful night
> They broke my bower and slew my knight,
> Just in my soft and longing arms
> Where I believed him free from harms,
> They pierced his tender gentle breast
> And left me with sad griefs oppressed.
> And was I not a weary wight,
> A maid, wife, widow all in a night?"
> — unknown

As of spring 1996 when he first came to see me, Edward MacDonald had never visited Scotland, ... at least not in this lifetime. The two-hour session of energy work and breathwork began with Edward relaxing, yet quickly experiencing lots of motion on his legs and especially his feet.

"I know I'm lying on this table, but I feel all kinds of anger ... seems to be centered around my feet," Edward wondrously described the sensation.

Through several minutes of coaching on breathwork and relaxation, I gradually eased Edward to a state where his body revealed vivid flashes of information from a cellular level.

He described many pictures, "I feel like I am at the top of the world; the mountains are so high, so beautiful! We love it here; all my clan does. Part of me is looking down on what appears to be a valley or a glen, the wind is pulling on my tartan, the sun is shining on steel," Suddenly, a deep frown covered his brow. "Something bad happened here, something awful...lots of killing."

Reassurance that he was now safe and in no danger, seemed to allow Edward to focus better. The energy and body's memories flowed more freely. "My right knee is going numb...wow, it's starting to ache. It hurts from the cold, from running...running away...fear...lots of fear. "

After several moments of Edward processing the energy, I asked him what else might he be aware of.

"Toy soldiers inside my knee...I see red-coated soldiers. Now, they're tartan plaid people running away. Scared!" Edward replied.

"Remember, Edward, these are only images as though you were watching a movie," I reminded him.

"Breathe circularly and let go of your controlling, logical mind."

"Screaming everywhere! Terrible confusion in the dark...God, it's cold now, bitter cold," Edward continued as I piled blankets on him.

His body calmed as readily as it had begun with the drama. "It's stopped; everything's totally dark now...no motion. My knee's okay too," he assured me. "I feel like something 'ugly' has left."

Ever so slowly, Edward MacDonald brought his consciousness back into the room. As he did so, I asked if he'd done any reading on the Massacres at Glen Coe. He looked bewildered, "What's Glen Coe?"

Thus began Edward MacDonald's unending quest into his family's past.

The author atop the Highlands of Glencoe

Bliaðna nan Caorach

The defeat of the Jacobite army in the Battle of Culloden in 1746 signaled the beginning of the end of the Highland way of life. The British government began deliberate efforts to break up Gaelic society. After Culloden no quarter was given. Hundreds of wounded Highlanders were shot to death, hung, bayoneted or burned alive. Through the proscription of kilts and tartans, as well as arms, the clan system began breaking up.

Government troops were sent out to the clan lands of those loyal to Prince Charles. Fugitives' homes were looted and burned, while their cattle were driven off and the countryside devastated. The campaign of attrition advanced in earnest April, 1746 as a special Disarming Act was passed by the British Government. The obvious intent to crush the Highlanders' spirit was more blatant. The bagpipes were even prohibited as an "instrument of war." So many facets of the Gaelic way of life seemed to offer a political and military threat to the British Government; these they saw fit to destroy in every manner possible. Already as early as the beginning of the 1700's the 42nd Highland Regiment or the Black Watch had been formed, an evolution from the Independent Companies raised by the Government to keep order in the Highlands.

Too, it was another face of the Lowlanders versus the Highlanders. 'Mi-run mor nan Gall' was the Lowlanders' expression of hatred for the Highlanders. This was a period when the Lowlanders of Scotland were acquiring romantic attachments to kilts and tartans while their Highland countrymen were being annihilated by soldiers.

The Highlander has always had an incredibly wonderful attachment to his native location. But after Culloden the Highland chiefs recognized themselves as landlords, no longer warlords. Their tenants and sub-tenants, also their clansmen, now had to pay rents. What previously had been paid by military support, now had to be paid in services leading to money.

The Year of the Sheep, "Bliadna nan Coarach," was 1792. The landowners found themselves midst appallingly difficult times; they became desperately concerned with making their estates pay. The Highlanders were deserted and betrayed by their chiefs as soon as they recognized that sheep farming would be the easiest method of achieving monetary gains on their estates. But large areas of land were necessary for this goal. Tenant eviction began as sheep became preferred to humans.

Some Gaels deemed it necessary to emigrate to North America; others enlisted in the new Highland regiments. While the clearances seemed heartless, there were a few chiefs who refused to do the same. MacLeod of MacLeod, Lord MacDonald, Robertson of Struan and MacKenzie of Cromartie aided the victims of their neighboring chiefs. The MacNabs emigrated to America, taking most of their clansmen along, whereas Lord Campbell of Breadalbane tried to prevent his clansmen from leaving the country.

In the late 17th century, Charles Chiswell who was recently immigrated from Scotland, became a prominent citizen of Williamsburg. It was his dream to settle a completely Scottish community in the "Virginia area." He was awarded a grant of 9,976 acres of land on which to build a castle and to establish Scotch Town.

Builders and artisans were transported directly from Scotland and enthusiastically began construction. As work progressed a terrible fever struck the community killing many. With that came the fear of the illness spreading further. The Scottish people fled back to their homeland.

In 1771 John Henry arrived from Scotland to resume building on a large portion of the Scotch Town land. Then later as his son Patrick Henry was Governor of Virginia, he lived on the estate while the Governor's Mansion was being completed in Williamsburg.

As early as 1685 the MacPhersons of Inverestrie had purchased 5,000 acres in Pennsylvania. The founder and Governor of Georgia transported 130 Highlanders from Inverness - shire to his colony, defending it against the Spaniards. North Carolina received 350 emigrants from Argyll in 1739. To the north Lochlan Campbell of Islay sailed to New York in the 1730's and arranged for the landing of several hundred more Scottish emigrants. Soon after that 200 MacKintosh clansmen of Borlum sailed to settle in Georgia. Too, one MacNeil chieftain from Barra lead 370 clansmen to North America. By the outbreak of the American Revolution 20,000 Scottish Highlanders had come to North America. These people would eventually participate in both sides of that conflict.

Colonel Allan MacLean was instrumental in forming the Royal Highland Emigrant Regiment which would wear the Highlander uniforms throughout the American Revolution. Yet another colorful unit was formed at the request of George III. The 71st Fraser Highlanders consisting of over 2,000 men were mustered my Simon Fraser and sailed for the continent to fight in the American War of Independence in 1775.

Allan MacDonlad and his wife Flora, such an important principal in the Jacobite Rebellion, had emigrated in 1772 to Cumberland County but remained loyal to King George. As the Revolution ended, the pair returned to their beloved Scotland, quite disillusioned with the American War of Independence.

Summer of 1819 the severe burnings midst the Highlanders began in earnest. Word reached the remaining tenants in advance, warning them. Yet, they couldn't believe the rumors until they were witness to it. In the distances the Highlanders watched the black smoke roll from small townships and crofts while the clearances moved even more severely in their direction.

A large degree of contemptuousness was involved in the burnings of family huts and moss timbers, the destruction of men, women, bairns of the clans, their livestock and potato patches which had filled their bellies. The claim was to be improving on a "slothful way of life," but in reality, they were creating lush pastureland for sheep.

The bards of the age felt great inspiration for their songs. With it came grim recognition of the beginning of the end of Gaelic society.

The Last Battle of the American Revolution

A decade before the American Civil War, three-fourths of the white population of the South was of Celtic descent. Similarly high figures were true of the North as well. The years of 1861-1865 were the bloodiest and most tumutuous days of America's history. Fathers and sons, brothers and brothers, Celtic warriors were all pitted against each other fighting for causes which were firmly held dear to their hearts. Each was prepared to pay the ultimate price to uphold their principles. And each, both Confederate and Union, had a belief in something fiercely great to be so ready to exit life so soon.

The Celtic heritage brought forth such leaders as Robert E. Lee, a descendant of Robert the Bruce and a Mason; Andrew Jackson, a Scotch-Irish arriving via Ireland; John Paul Jones; Sam Houston; "Stonewall" Jackson; Davy Crocket; General Patton; and a host more, including General Thomas F. Meagher. Those Celtic warriors, whether in blue or gray, established themselves early on as flamboyant and gallant heroes - for these were the Sons of Scotland and the Sons of Erin.

Nearly 200,000 Irish-born men served in the Union forces. More than twenty of those regiments were nearly 100% Irish. Sadly, the state of Virginia absorbed the blood of so many of these; more Irish blood was shed in Virginia than any other state.

Among the Confederate Army, General Patrick Cleburne, originally from County Cork, was outstanding as a commander. General Thomas "Stonewall" Jackson also was of both Scottish and Irish descent. The Irish Jasper Greens of Georgia were an active Confederate regiment. Present at Fredericksburg were a number of Confederate Irish companies, such as the 23rd Georgia, who partied with their Federal compatriots of the Irish Brigade the night before battle.

Those tragic years gave the Irish an opportunity to prove their worth before the eyes of a divided nation. But, the distinguished legacy of the famous Union Irish Brigade would establish them forever in history as they were seemingly always hurled into the hottest part of the fray.

From the shadow of a scaffold at Clonmeil jail in Ireland, a flamboyant Irish revolutionary with a fiery temper came to New York. Thomas F. Meagher, even in his native land, was dedicated to seizing freedom by the gun and by the sword. The Irish Brigade, as were thousands of other soldiers, was still fighting for freedom from oppression, segregation, and discrimination and fighting to uphold their Celtic heritage. General Meagher's Irish Brigade began as the 69th New York State Militia. At First Manassas in July, 1861 they were first given the opportunity to fight with distinction.

Celts on Parade

The streets of Broadway in New York City were lined by family members and well-wishers as they cheered the regiments going off to war. This pleasant day of May 23, 1861 was the setting for several flashy, flamboyant New Yorkers marching off to set records of valor and glory in history. Both the Scottish and the Irish reputation for military prowess was already highly respected. These soldiers would not disappoint.

Several troops of Zouaves marched ahead proudly in their, white havelocks, fezzes, and red trousers. Among these were the 146th New York. Soon the Duryée Zouaves (the 5th New York Regiment) could be determined midst all the bright colors. Present were James Murphy, born in Ireland; James Mahoney, born in Ireland; George Guthrie, born in Ireland; Carlile Boyd of Scotland, as well as many other brave men who would earn the reputation as "the red-legged devils, and a terror to 'evil-doers'". They were on their long, arduous trek leading them to fight in places such as Bull Run, Gaines Mill, Cold Harbor, Wilderness, Antietam, Marye's Heights, and Gettysburg.

Bagpipes skirled a Highland tune as the colorful outfits of the 79th New York Cameron Highlanders came into view behind the Zouaves. The Scottish Cross of St. Andrews was proudly displayed on their banner. Composed largely of Crimean War veterans later evicted from their native Scotland during the Highland clearances, this unit had already seen three years of militia experience. These fierce Celts were more professional than most of the Union regiments.

On October 8, 1858 Sir Roderick Cameron had verbalized his idea of establishing a Highland regiment. The idea was quickly solidified as the Queen's Own 79th Cameron Highlanders became the model for the American regiment. Wearing the Cameronian tartan kilts, colorful Glengarry (caps), navy-blue with red-trimmed jackets, sporrans, and kilt hose, the 79th New York would retain their identity through battles at Manassas, Secessionville, Chantilly, Antietam, and on through Tennessee.

Colonel James Cameron was commander of the 79th New York, leading his men up Henry House Hill to fight against "Stonewall" Jackson's Rebels at First Manassas. Here Colonel Cameron was killed; and Colonel Isaac Stevens took his place, but not until after a major 'low' in the 79th's morale. Stevens was elevated to higher command in October, 1861 at which time Colonel David Morrison assumed the position. Formerly an officer of the 42nd Highland Infantry (the Black Watch), Colonel Morrison proved himself to be an able commander.

The Last Letter Home

Just prior to the beginning of the Seven Days Campaign, June 25, 1862, Union forces had pushed to within seven miles of the Confederate capital at Richmond. General Robert E. Lee had assumed command and named his rebel forces the Army of Northern Virginia.

The 29th Massachusetts Infantry was attached to the Irish Brigade just before the Seven Days Campaign, giving Meagher's unit the standard number of four regiments. As battle advanced to Gaines Mills on June 26, the second day of the campaign, Stonewall Jackson's men were destroying the 9th Massachusetts. But before the rebels could succeed, the Irish Brigade reinforced their fellow Irishmen in thwarting their enemy.

Again, General Meagher's men fought fiercely as they were employed as the rear guard at Savage Station on the 29th and at White Oak Swamp on the 30th. For the sixth time in a week, 160,000 men of the two armies prepared to do battle fifteen miles southeast of Richmond. That day July 1, the 88th New York Regiment of the Irish Brigade would tangle with Lee's Louisiana Tigers, Irishmen in gray.

Meeting the fighting Irish at close range with no time to load muskets, the Tigers fought with bowie knives and pistols. Equally surprised by the encounter, the Irishmen had no time to fix bayonets. The 88th New York fought with a half-Gaelic, half-English scream, using their muskets as clubs. Long after dark as one of the Tigers' mounted officers was seized, the Louisiana troops lost heart and retreated.

All the Confederates fought valiantly. Rebel troops sheltered in a nearby stand of trees pinned down another company of the Irish Brigade. The Confederate commander directed the firing from his men with great accuracy. The Irishmen couldn't move.

Sergeant Driscoll, one of the best marksmen in the Irish unit, raised his rifle, took aim, and felled the Rebel officer. As the Confederates fled, Driscoll was instructed to see if the officer was dead.

"Father," was the word murmured by the officer as Driscoll turned him over. The Confederate's eyes closed forever. Driscoll's son had moved to the South before the war.

Minutes later, Driscoll's unit was ordered to charge. Driscoll soon fell as his body was riddled with bullets. Father and son were hastily buried in a single grave, with a rough cross, on the battlefield at Malvern Hill.

135 years later the reenactors of the 12th Virginia Infantry were present with other units to honor those who'd fought at Malvern Hill. Some of those gathered assumed that it would be a typical scenario of lamp tours through camp. Could the spectral soldiers who would welcome them be among those who died fighting against the Irish Brigade?

Henry Kidd, Sergeant with the 12th Virginia, describes events as they unfolded, "We were portraying camp life, a Living History, of the night before the battle. One of our boys was characterizing a Georgia boy of the 12th Virginia".

"The Georgia soldier had written a letter to his mother which our man was reading. Each time a different tour group came by stopping at our camp, the Georgia boy would read this poignant letter. The first two readings were devoid of emotion," explains Henry, "as were the last two. You could tell he was trying to show his feelings, but it was only overacting. However, the third time the letter was read, something special happened".

"'Dear Mother,' began the soldier. 'Taps' began playing somewhere in the distance, one of the most perfect versions of 'Taps' that I've ever heard," Sergeant Kidd describes. "They didn't miss a note; it was soft and slow as it should be played. During this reading of the letter, the boy's voice changed. It was truly as though he was the soldier talking to his mother for the very last time. It honestly didn't sound like the voice of the reenactor; he was so full of emotion."

Henry continues excitedly, "Everyone present was aware of the electricity in the air! One friend of mine in that tour group approached me later, shook my hand and exclaimed that the scene had given him cold chills. He said, 'Henry, I've got to tell you! This is the most real portrayal I've ever seen!"

Private Tim Fredrikson also a 12th Virginia member, approached Henry. Tim gently placed his hand on Henry's shoulder, "While our boy was reading his letter, there were fifteen dead Confederate soldiers standing behind us."

"After all the scenarios were completed," Sergeant Kidd continues, "Tim commented that he was strongly being drawn toward the treeline about 200 yards from us. Several men from our unit walked in that direction. We'd covered about a third of the way when all of us suddenly halted. The temperature had abruptly dropped about 15 degrees! There was no breeze blowing or other obvious cause for the temperature change. It had suddenly just dropped all around us."

Henry experimented for the group. "After I'd stopped walking, I moved out of that area 10-15 feet; the temperature was up to normal. Then I stepped back into the area, and the temperature dropped dramatically again. There was definitely another presence midst that cold spot."

A previously unidentified reenactor approached them from the distant camp. Sergeant Kidd and the others motioned him toward them. "When he arrived I asked him if he noticed any temperature change?" Henry explains, "That's all I said to him".

The Yank reenactor stretched his hand into the area and exclaimed, "Oh my God, they're here!" He knew instantly what the men of the 12th Virginia were experiencing. After identifying himself from the 5th New Hampshire unit, Dana drifted away from the assembly of men. He was well-aware that the spirits present were Confederate and he felt unwelcome.

"Private Fredrikson was still sensing a stronger presence toward the treeline." Henry continues, "So, I suggested that we move on. As we did we discovered another cold spot and lingered in the midst of it a while."

"Suddenly, I too felt a really strong pull toward the trees. I had to walk further in that direction, but slowly. Another peculiar sensation hit me just before the treeline," Sergeant Kidd recalls. "I could smell body odor. I knew it wasn't me, and there was no one visible within 50 feet of me. That distinct, strong odor really startled me. I stopped, looked around to see who was there. No one!" Henry repeated his previous experiment. "I stepped out of that spot and the smell was gone. When I stepped into it again, the body odor was present. Yet, it didn't linger long; it soon dissipated".

He was aware of a welcoming emotion, as opposed to one of anger. "I felt like the presence was glad that I was there, sort of like 'welcome to our ranks,'" he recalls.

Next, Henry became aware of a difference in the ground as he approached the wooded area. "I thought that I could see images differently, but I wasn't certain of what I was seeing about the ground. In fact," he rationalizes, "I even returned the next day in an attempt to disprove what I saw, yet I wasn't successful in that. In the treeline under the limbs of the trees where it is dark and the tree trunks are, and between that area and where the brushline starts, is a real dark area. That is the space where I saw silhouetted shapes of men's heads, shoulders and elbows bent back to their sides as though they were holding muskets centered in front of them. It wasn't one or two, but an entire regiment of Confederate soldiers from 135 years ago standing there in front of me!"

Henry, an exceptional Civil War period artist, describes the scene as only a talented person could, "Moving toward the regiment was like observing an Impressionistic painting. As I moved closer to them, I could no longer make out individual forms. If I stepped back, I could again see details. Yet, the entire area was illuminated with an unusual shadowy light". Henry then describes a most rewarding feeling, "I stood near the Confederate ranks and had the sensation of the soldiers closing in around me. 'Thanks!' was the clear message I felt from them."

"I left the spectral regiment behind and approached a small rise. There I was hit with another odor - that of peanuts. Around me was the breath of someone who'd been eating peanuts!" exclaims Henry. "I was aware of that odor more than once on my way back to my unit".

As Henry approached camp of the 12th Virginia, Tim was in the midst of conversation. Fellow - reenactors surrounded him. Henry again experienced the dramatic temperature drop that frequently accompanies an unknown entity. "I immediately felt the presence that was with Tim; the temperature had fallen about 15 degrees in that particular location". Henry goes on, "Another individual was speaking through Tim, the distinct voice of a southern youth. The soldier identified himself as a seventeen-year-old boy named Samuel Edmunds of Tazwell, Virginia. He had been one of two brothers in the same unit fighting for the Confederacy."

Henry's compassion for the frightened soldier is obvious as he continues describing what followed. "Samuel was afraid of dying the next day, as well as doubt as to whether or not he'd be able to 'do his duty.' His even greater fear was whether or not he would be accepted into Heaven if he was killed."

Other reenactors gathered around tried to console the youth. Yet, Samuel didn't seem to respond to them. It was Sergeant Kidd that he heard. "I began talking to him, saying 'Jesus Christ is with you'. Jesus is with you. You will be in Heaven forever. He that believeth in Him shall never perish, but have everlasting life.' It seemed as though the frightened soldier wanted and needed to hear that passage. Samuel began praying, and I prayed with him," recalls Henry. "Suddenly, something came over me and I started singing 'Dixie,' real slow and soft."

"The young soldier's voice joined me singing 'Dixie', gradually overpowering my voice," continues Henry. "It seemed as though the boy came to an understanding as to his religious beliefs in Christ and in God. He felt easier about the days to follow." Union reenactors would comment later that the voice echoed through the entire camp grounds.

Again, the reenactors felt drawn toward the treeline. Henry describes what followed, "Two of our men Whitt Smith and his son Christian walked slightly ahead. As we arrived at the slight rise where you could barely see the treeline, the ghostly unit was still visible and waiting. Whitt, the man foremost to arrive, proceeded toward them. I said, 'Whitt you're right there at them!' As he slowly stepped into the midst of them, the Confederate regiment parted ranks as if to admit a fellow soldier. Whitt turned facing me. As he did the color party for the regiment closed ranks around him, accepting him as a member."

Ending an evening of rewarding experiences, the men returned to camp. But before leaving the wooded area behind, Tim took one last look. He saw one lone, phantom Union soldier poised at the edge of the trees. Ira Bronson's face was not visible, yet the shoulder boards and much of his uniform were.

Later, Dana Tremblay of the New Hampshire unit, recalled his feelings as he was separating himself from the Confederate assembly. "I too was being drawn into the treeline. There were gray shapes in formation, tall to small, as reenactors line up in regimental formation." Dana, who is no stranger to metaphysical experiences, was quite active during the 1970's in exploring these phenomena. He continued his story, aware of what he was sensing, "As I stepped slightly into the edge of the woods, the cold spots enveloped me in a fog! The treeline seemed to disappear as though it had a shadowy feeling. 'We are so glad you are here,' was the message they sent me, 'also that of love.' I had the distinct impression of a Union officer standing directly in front of me, raising his sword in salute! Finally so very reluctantly I made myself leave the group."

Sunday, the next day Dana returned to that same area at high-noon. "The same cold area enveloped me in welcome".

"After returning home," Dana explained, "I did further research on our unit during that fight. I had been standing in the actual line of fighting where the 5th New Hampshire stood, which was the left flank of the northern army."

Dana also offered substantiating information to Tim. "The Union soldier you saw was Ira Bronson of the 5th New Hampshire. Ira had enlisted in 1861 as a musician and was present at the Battle of Malvern Hill. Later during the war, Bronson became a lieutenant with that unit". At that location near the edge of where those trees stand today, Tim had witnessed Bronson at the point of the right wing of the 5th New Hampshire as it fought 135 years ago.

Private Whitt Smith of the 12th Virginia also did some "homework" afterward. Whitt traveled to Fredericksburg in order to search extensive Civil War records. He discovered more verification for Tim —a Samuel Edmunds of 26th Virginia Infantry, Co. G; a Samuel Emons of 22nd Virginia Infantry, Co. B; and an S. Edmonds of the 5th Virginia Cavalry.

Dana Tremblay (right) with men of 5th New Hampshire at Fishers Hil, near Cedar Creek, VA.

Antietam

Martha and her husband had traveled from their home state of Alabama in four days to arrive at Antietam Battlefield on September 17, 1997. Her husband, Jack, was an avid Civil War buff, but Martha was fairly disinterested and unknowledgeable about the Civil War. From the bottom step in front of the Park Service plaque, Martha gingerly set foot into the Sunken Road. "Oh, dear heaven! What is this? What's happening to me?" she remarked while clutching at her chest. She suddenly felt herself immersed in a flood of tears. "I feel like I just stepped into a mass grave!" She was sobbing now, almost uncontrollably. Jack finally realized that she was seriously in distress.

He made it to her side, taking her by the elbow. "Here. let's get out of the lane." Jack steered his wife back to their car until she could pull herself together. She had no idea that she was walking into Bloody Lane on the 135th anniversary of the battle, at the hour when the heaviest casualties would have been lying dead.

Jack explained to her, "You were standing in the spot where four Alabama units fought and died. Colonel Gordon of the 6th Alabama Regiment had been wounded for the fifth time and was out of the fray. His adjutant had received orders to turn the regiment to face the Union forces who were on the move and firing into the lane. But the adjutant misinterpreted the order. Instead, he told his men to 'about face forward march, fall to the rear.' Consequently, the 4th Alabama Regiment to their left questioned if the order wasn't meant for them too."

General Lee's intentions in Maryland were to remove some of the pressures from the soils of war-ravaged Virginia. The combat erupted near Antietam Creek whose surrounding rolling terrain offered some wooded areas and a tall field of corn ready for harvest. All of which should have provided ample protection for Confederate defenses. Sunken Road, as it was then noted on military maps, served as a natural rifle pit for the southerners. The 7th West Virginia Infantry and Posey's Mississippi Brigade were positioned in the field in front of the sunken road.

The green flag, with its ancient golden Celtic harp blazoned upon it, burst though the early morning sunlight and was flapping in the breeze. The Irish Brigade had arrived and was leading the assault on the Confederates tenaciously trying to maintain a position in the old farm road. The Irishmen were leading Richardson's Division into battle, reinforcing the attack on Lee's center. This was the Green Isle soldiers' next major engagement after Malvern Hill.

A split rail fence blocked their forward charge. Several Irishmen sprang forward to tear down the obstacle. The Confederates poured deadly fire onto them and the advancing columns spilling through the fenceline. Still, the officers and men of the Irish Brigade surged forward. The four North Carolina regiments under Anderson's command fell in grotesque piles of death as the Irishmen advanced to within thirty paces of the sunken road, ever since referred to as Bloody Lane.

The fighting raged on for nearly four hours before confusion and sheer exhaustion finally ended it. The green flags of Erin were riddled with Confederate bullet holes. Eight color bearers of the 69th New York alone were killed or wounded, as one after another raised the banner again and again.

The courageous General Meagher, lying unconscious after his horse had been shot from under him, was carried off the field of fighting. At the end 540 casualties were declared from Meagher's Fighting Irish.

However, on this—the bloodiest single day in American history—other units were hotly engaged in their own tangles. Major General Hooker's Union First Corps tackled the Confederate left commanded by General "Stonewall" Jackson. The area surrounding the Dunker

Church was the prime objective. There were encounters through the East Woods, West Woods and various farms and cornfields. In Hooker's reports he wrote, "Every stalk of corn in the northern and greater part of the field was cut as closely as could have been with a knife, and the slain lay in rows precisely as they had stood in their ranks a few moments before".

At Antietam Creek itself, another scenario was being played out. The colorful and fierce Scottish Highlanders of the 79th New York found themselves in the thick of battle against Confederates. Remarkably, the Highlanders escaped with only forty casualties resulting from the fighting across Burnside's Bridge.

This afternoon of the 135th anniversary at Sharpsburg, I walked the length of Bloody Lane. I smelled the tobacco smoke of invisible men from years gone by. A slight breeze stirred the insects and birds, but I saw no mysterious apparitions—at least not until I reached the far end of the old sunken road, quite near the observation tower. In my hand I held a new tape recorder, purchased especially for this occasion. New batteries were loaded inside it. The recorder had worked perfectly all day as I walked the battlefield with Tim.

The bolt of energy that hit me coming from the direction of my right side nearly sent me reeling. The electrical charge zig-zagged from top-to-bottom, landing in the ground beneath my feet. The entire sensation lasted a very long five or six seconds, enough to make me catch by breath. When it was over, the cassette recorder and batteries were ruined. All the buttons jammed on the tape player and the batteries were dead.

Middlekauf Farm, slightly north of the Park Service Battlefield, was the location for the filming of the movie "Antietam." During the original engagement Middlekauf was utilized as a field hospital for wounded Union soldiers. But in July and September, 1997 it was littered with camps and tents of nearly two-hundred reenactors on site for the movie shoot. The energy was incredibly high that week, enough so that several men had difficulty sleeping at night.

Tim Fredrickson was one who got little rest that week. "We were okay until the third evening. Everyone sat around the campfires, singing, telling tales of the war, enjoying the comraderie," Tim explains. Suddenly, he felt an incredible compulsion to go straight toward the Middlekauf barn. "Guys, I gotta go," Tim told them. He headed immediately to it. Twenty yards from the entrance, Tim stopped dead in his tracks. "I began to hear the cries and the screaming!" It was terribly unnerving," he admits. As he walked closer near the structure, every nerve was tingling, every hair on the back of his neck was standing on end.

"I literally walked up to the main entrance to the barn, but stood at the side of the drive. I was witnessing a field surgery in operation. There was a doctor working on casualties—blood and gore everywhere," Tim vividly describes the scene, shaking his head in near disbelief. "I listened to the cries and pleadings of the wounded. What struck me the worst was the dull, grinding sound of the bone saw." The whole scene lasted about forty-five minutes. Tim was mesmerized by it all, "I just sat there watching so intently; then suddenly it was gone. Suddenly nothing! I could still feel the energy, but no sounds or scenes".

He left the barn area and walked into camp. Barely beyond the edge of campfires, another reenactor, one who was truly a 'doubting Thomas,' approached Tim. "Man, are you okay?" the guy asked him.

"I guess so, why?" Tim wondered.

"Your face is as white as my shirt!" the fellow replied.

Tim looked down at his hands. They too seemed to have drained of all color. He spent another restless night with little sleep.

The fourth day was busily filled with shooting more scenes. On Middlekauf Farm the production crew had reconstructed the Dunker Church where the day after the battle, a truce had been agreed on by both Federal and Confederate sides so that the dead and wounded could be carried from the field.

After dinner that evening, another fellow-reenactor sought Tim out to say, "Hey, you've got to go over to the ladies in 'Wardrobe.' Those people had something pretty fantastic happen today."

Tim's curiosity was piqued. Right away he marched over to the 'wardrobe' building which happened to be one of the original

Middlekauf structures, a single-story outbuilding with a high, gabled roof. All the 'wardrobe' staff was present as Tim inquired of their experience.

"We'd been sitting here cutting out fabric and sewing on the truce flags for today's scenes," one woman spoke up. "Next thing we hear this loud 'Drip'! Everybody looked in the direction of the sound. And we saw this big drop of blood that'd landed on that cloth on top of that box over there," the woman nodded in the direction of which she spoke.

They each watched as Tim examined the piece of fabric. Indeed, it was blood, and nowhere could be found a logical source for it. Everyone present felt that its source originated 135 years ago. Nearly the entire grounds of the farm would have been soaked in blood from the dead and wounded. Virtually all of the outbuildings had housed thousands of Union casualties.

Bivouac of the Dead

The muffled drum's sad roll has beat
The soldiers' last tattoo.
No more on Life's parade
Shall meet that Brave and fallen few.
On fame's eternal camping ground
Their silent tents are spread
While glory guards with solemn realm
The Bivouac of the Dead.

No rumors of the foe's advance
Now swells upon the wind.
No troubled thoughts at midnight haunts
Of loved ones left behind.
No visions of the morrow's strife
The Warrior's dreams alarm.
No bragging horn nor screaming fife
At dawn shall call to arms.

Their shivered swords are red with rust;
Their plumed heads are bowed.
Their hauty banners trailed in dust
Are now their martial shroud.
And plentious funeral tears have washed
The red stains from each brow.

And those proud forms by battle gashed
Are freed from anguish now.

The neighing troop, the flashing blade
The bugle's stirring blast, the charge,
The dreadful cannonade,
The din and shout are past.
No war's wild note nor glory's peal
Shall thrill with fierce delight
Those breasts that never more may feel
The rapture of the fight.
Rest on in bond and sainted dead
Dear as the blood you gave.
No impious footsteps here shall tread
The herbage of your grave.

Nor shall your glory be forgot,
While fame her record keeps.
Our honor guards the hallowed spot
Where valor proudly sleeps.
Yon marble minstrel's voiceless stone
And deathless song shall tell
When many a vanished age has flown
The story how ye fell.
Nor wreck, nor change , nor winter's blight
Nor time's remorseless doom,
Shall dim one ray of glory's light
That guilds your deathless tomb.

by Theodore O'Hara
at Marye's Heights, 1858

Faugh A Ballagh

President Lincoln was displeased with McClellan's performance at Antietam, as the Commander had not pursued the Confederates' retreat after that battle. Consequently, Major General Burnside was chosen to replace him as the commander of Union forces. This transfer of officers would soon lead to one of the most famous battles of the Civil War.

November 15, 1862 Burnside set in motion 120,000 Federal troops to converge on Fredericksburg, Virginia. Their eventual goal was to capture Richmond beyond. As the Army of the Potomac reached the Rappahanock River late November, the men could have easily waded across and taken the city. But Burnside was firmly set on his arrangements to build pontoon boats for crossing. The four grand divisions under Sumner, Hooker, Franklin and the reserves under Sigel would make camp and wait. The 79th New York Highlanders, part of Sigel's reargaurd, would not see action in the days to come.

The Irish Brigade established its winter quarters midst the Falmouth hills and meadows. By this time the 28th Massachusetts and the 116th Pennsylvania had joined Meagher's men. The 28th Mass. was predominantly an Irish regiment from Boston. Whereas, the 116th PA, recruited in Philadelphia, were Irish immigrants and native-born Germans. Evenings around the campfires, the 7th Michigan Infantry sang songs like "John Brown's Body" and "All Quiet Along the Potomac." Duryee's Zouaves also were camped on the Henry farm outside Falmouth. The 5th New Hampshire was not far away.

There was surprising comraderie amongst the soldiers who would soon commit murderous firing upon each other. Both sides experienced scarcities of supplies. Picket lines were crossed by Yanks and Rebs alike to exchange "nips" of whiskey, tobacco, and coffee. Relatives and old friends from Ireland established a temporary peace until the butchery resumed. And one thing was certain, the Irishmen could always be counted on for a good party and a dram of whiskey even on the eve of the worst of battles.

As weeks passed on, Lee moved every available man to the heights overlooking the town. The Confederates refused to surrender Fredericksburg. Lee anchored his left line on Marye's Heights, a sloping hill with a low stone wall just below the military crest of the hill. The sunken road behind that wall would soon prove to be a perfect, natural rifle pit for the Rebels. The Union troops sat on the eastern side of the Rappahanock River and watched as the Confederates built more earthworks and rifle pits. Many men of the Irish Brigade, including Father Corby, were convinced that their generals would not lead them directly into the Confederate fire, so carefully prepared and reinforced.

Carole and Nathan were excited about moving into their new home. Fredericksburg is such a charming, historic city; and the newly constructed townhouse was going to offer the couple a splendid setting in which to reestablish their partnership. Situated on the east bank of the Rappahanock River directly across from downtown Fredericksburg and Marye's Heights, the home is located between the Chatham Bridge and the railroad bridge. Just beyond the railroad bridge sits the boyhood home of George Washington. Their unit, an end one, was completed before any others of the housing development begun in 1996.

The first night as they tried to sleep in the new surroundings, activities erupted. Raucous thumping, banging and men's voices in the dark kept them awake. "We heard so many loud noises that we thought teenagers were camping in the unit under construction beside ours," Carole declares. "The intense odor of smoke and fire coming from that direction alarmed us in such a way that we were concerned about them burning the place down!"

Several weeks passed as daily completion advanced on the adjoining home. As Nathan saw the sheet rock being installed, he checked with their future neighbors. No one had been inside the condominium at night. Nothing was disturbed, nor had any fires been lit. Nathan suspected that things were amiss, yet he didn't wish to alarm his wife. 'Surely, now that their new neighbors were moving in, matters would settle down,' he hoped.

Instead, they escalated. Muffled sounds of men's voices became louder, yet the exact words were indistinguishable. Tapping sounds became more prevalent. "I could hear the various cadences of conversations," Nathan explains. "It was beginning to sound like officers talking to enlisted men. Carole or I would be alone in a different part of the house and would hear conversations. Both of us assumed that the other was talking. Then we'd turn around to find ourselves alone. This occurred frequently for two months before either of us mentioned it."

Carole who is a lighter sleeper that Nathan experienced vivid, nightly awareness. "I'd wake up to the smell of heavy campfire smoke. Horses' harnesses creaking was incredibly distinct, as well as sounds of horses stamping and moving around. I heard the clink of bridle metal with chains, and gun magazines being worked on."

Then early in the day, Nathan began hearing cannons and guns firing somewhere off through the distance, somewhere through time...

3:00 A.M. on Dec. 11, 1862 Mississippi Rebs opened fire on the first wave of Federal pontoons launched into the river. Union fire responded from twenty-nine batteries; one-hundred, fifty cannons unleashed 8,000 projectiles onto Fredericksburg. The city was on fire! Combined with the early morning mists, the red sheets of flames and smoke made the town seem like a surrealistic painting.

About 6:30 A.M. the 5th New York Zoaves heard the call to "fall-in." They began their march on the Falmouth road. Still these Celts would be kept east of the river until the 13th. Here they made camp overlooking the river.

Volunteers from the 7th Michigan Infantry and the 19th and 20th

Massachusetts ferried across the river and battled Mississippi and Florida troops until darkness when they fled. Burnside now controlled Fredericksburg. On Dec. 12th Meagher's Irishmen packed up field rations and ammunition. The 1,200 Sons of Erin marched into the city to join other Union troops massed for assault.

General Lee observed the activities calmly. Burnside was maneuvering his men just as Lee had hoped, and Barksdale's men had bought precious time for Stonewall Jackson's troops to advance en masse against Burnside's forces.

Nathan often caught images of soldiers in his peripheral vision while inside their home. "The activities of military camp life accelerated in the summer 1996. Sometimes I smelled popcorn prepared over an outdoor fire, then tobacco smoke," he describes the sensations. "At first it seemed as though we had a problem with our ventilation system until we learned that no one nearby smoked at all. Sometimes the pipe smoke was as though the person was sitting beside me. What was really awful though was the foul smell of decaying bodies, rotting flesh, the smell of death all around. Then once in a while, we'd smell sweet jasmine mixed in with it, a wonderful scent."

Carole describes a small white dog which has often kept her company. "He's around me a lot here in the house and even accompanied me shopping at least one other trip out in my car. The image of him fades in and out from time to time." The couple have no pets of their own, but feel that the dog might have been a troop mascot.

"We have an old-fashioned, seven-day clock with Winchester chimes. This is a clock with a heavy 'tip' which can be heard throughout our four-story home. This clock and its chimes are supposed to be wound frequently. However, during these periods when the psychic activity is high, that clock will run for weeks without us winding it," Carole explains. "Then as the other energies are rampant, the clock won't chime on the hour, but will chime at odd times. Once the psychic phenomena die down and the tapping stops, the clock will be fine for a while. It'll even go through stages where it seems to be winding down slowly like it's ready to quit. Suddenly. it'll perk up and run for days without us touching it."

Another clock which was given to them as a gift, has its own life. Nathan explains, "This small battery-operated clock has never stopped running. Its pendulum swings constantly. Neither Carole nor myself has ever put a battery in it; it's empty and running on air. During the times of strongest electrical, psychic energy, that clock would also ring." Nathan shakes his head in mystery, "We finally put it away. That was too eery for us to handle!"

Sewing is Carole's favorite hobby. One evening as she and Nathan were relaxing at home, Carole put down her needle. The two of them stared in astonishment as it spun around to stop facing the opposite direction. Ten more times, Carole picked it up and replaced it with the needle repeating the sequence.

Nathan tells of another mystery. "We have a swinging door between two rooms closest to the central stairway, and the hinges on it are plenty loose. Yet, periodically that door will be nearly impossible to open. When that happens we both get the distinct impression that someone is on the other side pushing against us! As a matter of fact, some of the most intense of these occurrences are focused around this central staircase in the center of the home built from the ground floor up through the loft on the fourth level.

"When Nathan isn't home, quite often I'll feel like I have an unseen visitor," Carole says. "There'll be the slight draft created as someone moves past me. Usually, it preceeds the odor of tobacco or a sort of sweetness; some mornings it'll be the terribly strong odor of garlic!"

The loft in the top level is Nathan's office. While working there alone, he often hears people moving about in the next room - sounds of people sitting down and closing doors. Nathan sets aside his work, goes to check on the noise. It stops just when he gets to the next room. When he leaves the sounds resume. There are times when the events are so vivid that he feels himself turn white.

One night in April of 1997, Carole went to bed before her husband. "I layed down in bed but wasn't asleep. Suddenly, I was aware of something sit down on the side of the bed. Just prior to the actual impression on the mattress, I heard a sound like a dry leaf floating down from above. The next sensation was as though a heavy weight was on my chest! I could hardly breathe for several minutes. Then it disappeared!" Carole exclaims.

December 13th dawned cold, damp, and misty. The Zouaves had a thick smokey fog hanging about their camp, dimming the view of Fredericksburg. The men were lively, well - rested, and in good spirits singing while preparing breakfast. Soon they heard the distant cannonade from the city as the haze began to lift. From their eastern hillside vantage point, the 5th New York had an excellent view of battle preparations. Not before later that afternoon would these Celts join across the river.

The Irish Brigade had fallen in line, waiting for orders shortly after sunrise. Meagher's pronounced Gaelic voice could be heard issuing orders. Because the units' flags were absent for repairs, the commander ordered that sprigs of evergreen be placed in every man, including officers,' caps to emphasize their Irish heritage. "Faugh A Ballagh," the Gaelic motto of the 28th Mass. on their Green Flag proudly "Cleared the Way." The Irishmen moved out.

By noon a brigade of blue-coated men filed out of Fredericksburg. As quickly as they left the city, their battle lines were formed. Before them lay a canal with Marye's Heights just beyond. The charge of the stone wall was on!

The wall proved to be a formidable defense for the Confederates. From behind its shelter, Confederate artillery sent the souls of Federal patriots ascending to their Maker. North Carolina troops, Kershaw's South Carolina Brigade, and Cobb's Georgia Brigade, primarily Irish immigrants, defended the wall at Marye's Heights. Cobb's soldiers recognized with dismay their fellow-countrymen. "Oh, God, what a pity! Here comes Meagher's fellows!"

Still, the Celtic warriors rushed into the murderous fire. The 5th New Hampshire followed directly behind them. Colonel Cross, the flamboyant commander of the New Hampshire boys, was wounded and trampled by Union soldiers, his distinctive red bandanna remained intact. Throughout the day Burnside sent wave after wave of infantry to the slaughter. The fighting continued until darkness. Seven Union divisions had charged that hill in fourteen attempts. But not one of their men ever reached the stone wall.

Nathan and Carole have now done their "homework" after two years of phenomenal activities in their house. The Irish Brigade did camp on their property previous to marching into town. As the Rappahanock River floods nearly every year, the flood level rises 20-30 feet. The river did so during the war. It stands to reason that these soldiers had to camp above the flood level.

Originally, there'd been a house connected with the land on which they've built. This older house was used as a field hospital during the Fredericksburg engagement. Nearby on this property, the bodies of the slain Federals were piled three-deep. As many as 2,000 dead lay there at one time.

Wilderness 'Experience'

Celtic warriors in blue turned out full force at the Wilderness May 5-6, 1864. The 79th New York Highlanders left Tennessee, marched to Annapolis, Maryland, and in the spring moved overland to join the Army of the Potomac, Grant's campaign in the dismal forest of the Wilderness in Virginia. The New York Zouaves fought Ewell's Second Corps across Saunders Field, while the Irish Brigade fought Confederates on the Orange Plank Road. Afterward, in the area known as the Mule Shoe, the 116th Pennsylvania led the Union charges.

By the end of the month, what remained of Lee's and Grant's forces continued encounters at Spotsylvania and the North Anna River. Then on May 31 through June 3 the two armies clashed in another devastating arena—Cold Harbor.

Not only did the 5th New York Regiment stand mightily, but the 164th New York was also there. It was Colonel McMahon's brave men, one totally Irish unit of the war, who fell so riddled with bullets near the Confederate trenches at Cold Harbor.

Modern-day Civil War reenactors often gather in commemoration of these past battles, either in Living History Programs or recreations of the original fighting. One Virginia regiment, primarily based in Richmond, was one unit among several portraying its role at the Battle of Cold Harbor.

Richard tells of his experiences and his two-year comraderie with a Confederate soldier from the dead. Eventually, he would save Richard's life at the Wilderness. "We arrived at Cold Harbor late afternoon one Friday in Spring of 1996. As were several Federal and Confederate reenactors, we set up for a weekend Living History Program. I was informed in the evening that a guy named Joey was coming from out of town and that he would arrive late. Mine was the only tent with room for another person," Richard explains. "So Joey would be sleeping with me."

That first night was a cold one; and Richard, who's usually a very sound sleeper, had a restless night because of it. "I got up about 3:00 A.M. to use the bathroom," he continues. "It was a clear night; the moon was out. I was standing behind my tent and looked over to my left. There was a Confederate soldier standing not far away. I could make out a lot of details about his uniform. I assumed it was one of our men. He just stood there, staring straight ahead. I spoke to him casually."

No response—the guy didn't even turn his head.

Richard spoke to him again, "Well, I think you're as rude as hell." Still, no response. So, Richard returned to his tent, forgetting about the incident, and fell asleep.

A few hours later, Richard woke up again, for no apparent reason. "I looked over toward the tent flap and saw a guy sitting there. 'Hey, Joey, why don't you lay down? Why're you sitting there like that? Aren't you cold?'" Again, Richard could see the same details of the uniform as the moonlight filtered into the tent and the fire's embers offered a little glow.

Still, no response from his company.

From then Richard drifted in and out of sleep. Once more he halfway sat up, remarking to the soldier who was obviously not sleeping, "Look, buddy, we got a long day ahead tomorrow, and Sunday's Living History. Lay back down and go to sleep."

Sometime before dawn Richard barely roused himself from sleep another time. "I finally saw this guy lie down, and I felt him lie down too. I even heard the hay crumple when he moved. I thought no more of it and afterward slept soundly."

The following morning everyone was up early. Even Richard's visitor had vacated his tent. There was no extra blanket, nor bedroll.

The hay wasn't even disturbed. As of yet, Richard wasn't suspecting anything terribly unusual. And at that point he certainly did not believe in ghosts. "I made a fire and fixed coffee...couldn't see Joey anywhere, "Richard explains. "I asked my friends, 'Where's Joey? He was in the tent last night'."

"No, he wasn't. Joey never showed up," the others assured him.

"Now, I started getting the 'willies,' Richard started to feel something strange about the incident. "Well, somebody did. Who came in my tent last night?" He searched the faces of his friends for an explanation. "Who's playing games with me?"

Each man assured him that they weren't doing that. "None of us were in your tent. We were 'dead to the world."

"Yeah, he did! Joey slept in my tent last night. I guess he got cold and went home," Richard decided on the only logical explanation. But deep inside Richard began piecing together the parts. Gradually, he was to realize that who he saw was not any living human from their unit.

Shortly after Cold Harbor but before the Wilderness, the startling dreams began... "We're standing in woods, lots of smoke everywhere. It's a battle but without sounds of cannons. The two of us are standing together, both in Confederate uniforms. He's communicated that his name is William. He just stares at me. I'm so familiar with his face now. I've had this same dream many times," Richard recalls it vividly from memory. "I've searched every Civil War book I can get my hands on, looking for his face. I just want to be able to touch it."

Todd, another reenactor in Richard's regiment, was present at the Wilderness two weeks later, in May. "Friday afternoon we dug trenches. That night with our entire company present, we slept on a high peak. What a rainy, cold, miserable night that was-out in the open without tents," Todd describes the scene. "Late that night, well after everyone was in bed, I was suddenly wakened by the terrible screaming of a man. 'I'm gonna kill you! I'm gonna kill you!'"

One of the guys in their regiment, bayonet in hand, was lunging at Richard's heart. The private's eyes were wide open, yet he didn't seem to heed the other men. Todd saw one man with a cigarette lighter, flicking it trying to see what was happening. "The fire was dying out, so the lighter created a really weird strobe-light effect," Todd recalls.

"But I could see the crazed look in this man's eyes. He truly intended to kill Richard right then and there!"

Richard grabbed the man's arm and reached back with his right hand to hit the guy, "I yelled, 'What the hell's wrong with you!?' This private's still screaming at the top of his lungs about killing me. Geez, it was weird and scary! We were all mystified as to what was going on."

Finally, the crazed reenactor came to his senses. Shaking his head in disbelief, he apologized repeatedly. "I know my eyes were wide open, but I was asleep having this awful nightmare!" The guy attempted an explanation. "There were three Yankee soldiers trying to drown me in a stream. Two of 'em held my head under water, but the third one who was with them was laughing at me while the others pushed my face under water. Instead of striking out at the two trying to drown me, I wanted to kill the Yank laughing while I was dying!"

The others in the regiment settled down for the night. Unfortunately, Richard wasn't to be calmed so easily. He went over and stoked up the campfire. There he remained the entire night, staring into the embers. "To this day I know that my friend William saved my life. I'm such an extremely sound sleeper that it takes a real effort on someone's part to wake me up. That night before I was stabbed, a hand reached out and vigorously shook me by the foot to waken me. I can still feel it! It was pitch dark, but I sensed that I needed to move. Suddenly, I was on my feet. I am positive it was my 'friend' from Cold Harbor." Richard is certain that it was also him who paced beside his bedroll the remaining hours until dawn. Off in the distance of the night's cover, Richard could also see phantom Union soldiers drilling—possibly those Celtic regiments from so many years previous?

Not so long after his Wilderness adventure, Richard's regiment again traveled to Cold Harbor. "I hadn't talked about these things much because I didn't wish to be made a fool of," he explains. "But so much has happened with William, including the continuing dreams, that I have to find out more information."

Two more reenactors in the regiment became more than curious about Richard's experiences. At their second trip to Cold Harbor, the two were determined to 'see something for themselves.' These guys followed me around constantly all weekend," Richard says. "That night after everyone else was asleep, I felt someone tugging on my feet. I sat up and saw William standing nearby. But as soon as a few other people began stirring, William was gone."

Another location where William was visible was at Malvern Hill in the summer of 1996. Richard recalls, "I saw him hanging around camp some, off and on but with no other activities." The vivid dreams, as well as personal incidents with his Confederate companion, have continued for nearly two years.

However as of December, 1997, circumstances altered dramatically when William began appearing at Richard's home. "One day close to Christmas, he manifested by sitting in a rocking chair upstairs in my bedroom. Another day soon after that, I was reading a magazine article about the Wilderness Battle to a friend over the phone," he says. "All of a sudden, I had this dramatic tingling sensation crawling up the back of my neck! I knew something was going on, as I glanced at a Kunstler picture hanging on the wall. I always kept a Confederate flag draped at its side. Two days later, that flag had been removed from the edge of the picture. I found it draped over my reenactor's uniform upstairs in my bedroom!

"My wife swore she never touched it,nor had anything to do with it, " Richard checked out the only two possibilities. "My stepdaughter denies knowing anything about it. Pretty soon after the flag episode, I also realized that my boots had been put beside the uniform too."

Richard's dreams about William increased now to twice a week. Their contents began to intensify. The two soldiers stood face-to-face in a wooded location enveloped in smoke. Richard describes their interaction, "As the dreams unfolded, I could see that William has tears in his eyes as he pushes me away. I look down at my chest and can see blood covering the front of me." Richard recognizes William as his best friend throughout the war until his own death at the Battle of the Wilderness.

"I'm lying on the ground, shot, looking up at William and then looking away," he resumes. "William is quite emotional and is telling me, 'no one is going to get you; I'll be back. I won't let the rodents get you. I promise I'll be back.' Then he disappears as he's ordered to follow his regiment."

The dreams became so frequent and so emotionally intense for Richard. Finally out of desperation, he shouted out to William in his last dream, "You did what you 'had' to! You don't owe me anything! It's okay."

With these remarks from his long-lost friend, William seemed to receive the release he so desperately had searched for. The soldier faded away, waving good-bye, never to return.

Photo taken on June 2, 1994 by the author. Image of Union soldier who died in Confederate trenches at Cold Harbor, probably one of 164th New York.

Following the Plume

Major General James Ewell Brown Stuart is a fine example of a natural leader which Scotland produced for America. Born in Patrick County, Virginia and descended from Bonnie Prince Charlie, J.E.B. Stuart came to us with superb leadership qualities, as well as his ability to inspire men. His charisma and tact enabled him to quickly resolve any issues that occurred between his men. But, the men who served on Stuart's staff were noted for their devotion to him and to each other.

May, 1861 JEB Stuart was newly commissioned and was immediately put in charge of the cavalry forces under Colonel Jackson's command. By July of 1861, Stuart had been made a full colonel, Commander of the 1st Virginia Cavalry. Among his many attributes, JEB Stuart had a rare gift of insight into peoples' talents. Forty-eight men were hand-picked by him and served as his loyal staff members until his fall at Yellow Tavern May 11, 1864.

Lost are the names and deeds of many of his faithful men. However, the memories of one scout and soldier who followed Stuart's plume, comes to us today through the voice of a present-day Civil War reenactor. Heather Heal was born in England. Her grandmother was born into the Yule family, a sept of the Buchanan Clan. For countless years Heather has felt as though she was one of JEB Stuart's most loyal cavalrymen. Today Heather is a reenactor with 9th Virginia Cavalry, Co.B.

October 30, 1996 Heather began her first Breathwork Therapy session with me. "There's a double image of me on the table, then in woods on a horse. Feels like I'm floating. I see myself scouting, wearing grey in Civil War, tall, dark hair, mustache. The pain in my left knee is more prominent...soldier kneeling on left knee," Heather vividly began experiencing scenes, as well as physiological sensations. "He frequently bent down on that knee; as he stood up the pressure went away. Knelt that way in habit to shoot and draw maps, a favorite position of his. Now, my throat's getting scratchy."

Heather could see herself as one of JEB Stuart's men, standing over him as he died at Yellow Tavern. As James MacFarlane, she rode with Stuart throughout the war. "James said he was from mountains and woods, not the shore. That was from a Revolutionary War lifetime."

She began crying over the loss of life, "I've been with him since the beginning, Manassas...JEB Stuart."

I attempted to reassure her and asked her, "What needs to be said to Stuart...any thoughts or emotions that you might not have said then at Yellow Tavern?"

"Only that he was a brave soldier, and was loved so very well," she responded. "I'm seeing a lot of anger toward the Yankees...betrayal!"

I couldn't resist a comment, "Well, you're fighting a war. That has a lot to do with anger." We both laughed at the idea.

"He's not to be blamed for Gettysburg," Heather continued. "He did do the honorable thing."

"What might Stuart say to you and other people around him?" I wondered. "Don't force it; breathe deeper and relax further."

"Forgiveness, they were all honorable men. So, let's reconcile, forgive them all," she offered.

"Sure. Forgiveness can be the most powerful healing too," I reminded her.

"He reminds us not to hate the Yankees, but to love them. They were men of honor too," Heather continued.

Then I asked her to do just that, "Can you do that now in your heart, also in your mind and body? Begin in your heart and pull out that forgiveness for them."

Thus began a deep emotional release for Heather. Much pain and grief were evident in her tears. Then she began shivering.

I reminded her not to control the emotions, but to let them flow freely. "Allow yourself to feel. That's what this is all about. Are you cold?"

"Yes! I'm freezing!" she exclaimed as I piled blankets on her.

Several more minutes of shivering and tears followed before she spoke again, "A flashback to New Mexico...after the war...I'm wearing the blue uniform...we had gotten into an argument, me and one of my fellow soldiers...over the Civil War, over who was right and who was wrong. This was someone who'd fought for the Yankees. He hated the Confederates. He shot me in the temple. As I was lying there dying, he came over to me and asked me to forgive him, that the war was over. I can see myself as the blood is flowing. I'm saying that I forgive him, letting go of the anger. Seeing those surroundings all around the mountains...I think I was a lieutenant, second lieutenant. I don't know if it's names I've heard or names that I've used, or maybe that's why I've used them before."

"You're trying to analyze the process now," I interjected.

Heather laughed, "I know. I know. The rational brain doesn't want to let go."

I reminded her that it takes some practice.

"I'm getting the name James MacFarlane," she said. "For some reason the name is important to me."

"That's definitely a Scottish name," was my comment.

"In this lifetime, I came from Scottish ancestry, and they say the soul chooses before it returns," she stated.

"What sensations do you have in your knee now?" I wondered.

Heather replied at first, "The pain is throbbing if I concentrate on it." Then after a pause, "For the most part, the pain is gone; it's totally gone."

"What about your head?" I next asked.

"Better, I don't feel the pain now, nor the blood," she was happy to say.

"And how about your throat?" I next had her check.

"That knot's gone. It was from the deaths and all the strong emotions," she readily identified them.

"That's understandable," I said. "Men are taught to hold their feelings in, to be stoic."

Heather responded, "Oh yes! You don't cry; you have to be macho. I've had problems with that in this lifetime too. I was almost suicidal once because I wouldn't let myself cry, because it's not the macho thing to do."

"Okay, let's really focus on the breathing and letting go of analysis." I didn't want us to get too far away from the information she was 'seeing.'

"There's someone else there, not Stuart...looking at a map," she slowly resumed. "I feel strongly that it's a map of Chancellorsville! Ross was there, he's one of my favorite people, but there's a group of men. I can't really see who they are, but the man who comes through strongest has grey...er dark hair with a lot of grey in it."

"It's important not to force this; 'let' your body experience the scene," I reminded her.

Heather continued, "I'm showing him the roads through the Wilderness area...where the Confederates are versus where the Federals are. I'm trying to make a point, but they're not listening to me."

"Why do you think they're not listening to you?" I inquired.

"How dare a sergeant tell us what to do! We're the generals! We know what to do!" she answered for them.

I could only wonder out loud, "Would it have made a difference in the outcome of the fighting if they'd listened?"

"James believed it at the time, but I'm getting flashbacks to Yellow Tavern," she said. "Stuart's telling him that it wouldn't have mattered, that Stuart was in charge. So...it was Chancellorsville. Stuart was in charge of the troops. He's telling James, 'I know you are upset; but it didn't matter. Either way would have been right.' I feel at peace with that. That's what he wanted...what Stuart wanted James to know...more than just forgiveness. 'Let go of the anger toward the superiors, as well as the frustration. You did your job. James, you're very headstrong and you kind of balk against authority...like Heather does now'."

"Ah yes, there's that Celtic blood rising—a Celtic warrior through and through," I observed. We both got a good laugh over the idea.

"I feel like Stuart's laughing too, as if to say, 'they may be generals but they know what they're doing'…most of them anyway, sort of tongue-in-cheek.

"I feel like a burden has been lifted off my shoulders," she noticed. "Yes, my shoulders feel light! If the bosses knew what they were doing, the others would be able to see 'why' and to forgive them, even if there's some anger there…not to be so angry at them…to be able to forgive them. I feel like that's related directly to what we're going through now at work.

"The more I study the Civil War and the honor that they had in doing their duty, the more I learn what it meant to be honorable and to earn their respect. I took those traits myself. The more I learn about James, the more I learn about Heather. Those two lifetimes are intertwined more than any other.

"I enjoy being home in my beloved Virginia, even though I don't live there now," she laughed. "But, I will…sooner or later! I'm coming home sometime."

"Apparently, there are some things to accomplish or learn where you are," I guessed.

Heather continued, "I was supposed to move to Lebanon, first, then Gettysburg. Had to find myself at Gettysburg …more so the second day of battle, even though we weren't there. We didn't make it 'til the evening of the second day; then we got chewed out for being late!"

Several moments passed while Heather tried to relax more and focus on centering herself. Then she spoke, "For a moment there, I saw a man…at least it looked like a man…there's nothing left in Virginia for him. He looks so sad. The house was dowsed in blood with their murder when the battle began. Men were scattered."

I sensed her tensing against the scene and emotions. "Try to relax and let James feel the emotions."

Heather continued slowly, "Some of the family is dead, but I see some relatives…much happiness even if the homestead's gone. The people are saved. Dad wants him to be a farmer." Heather thought that was funny. "I can't do that…don't have the patience for it. I'm ready for adventure. There's a whole world out there to explore, even if it does mean donning the hated Yankee uniform." She laughed more at this notion.

"I had a sweetheart," Heather, speaking for James, continued. "She couldn't wait though. She married another; she's a farmer's wife now. That's not for me…too big a world out there."

As we wound down her session, Heather realized that her left knee had stopped hurting completely. As for information on James' friendship with JEB Stuart, she seemed quite pleased. We agreed to meet again on a later date.

December 13, 1996 she met with me for her second Breathwork Therapy session. At this time Heather reported her experiences regarding her left knee. "When I left here last time, I was able to hike Culp's Hill with no pain at all during it or after. But, I still went for my regular physical therapy session later. They 'insisted' on again using the electrical shock treatment on my knee. Needless to say, that really started it hurting all over again!".

Thus, we commenced the session. "I'm in Scotland, early A.D. but I'm not Scottish; I'm Roman."

"Tell me what you see," I gently inquired.

"Just the mountains…but before I started going under, before I went to Scotland, I went back even further. Fast flashes! I was back…and um…I hate going back to this place," Heather was breathing quite heavily at this point.

By now what had been moderate pain in her left knee, was subsiding to only a little. I did several minutes of Reiki energy on it, helping it further. At the same time, I encouraged Heather to let go of the breathing pattern more.

"That's Heather imposing on…brother back then 'cause he thought he was doing the right thing, including this that they called Judas with others injurious," she observed.

I wonder "Where are you now?"

"Palestine," she replied. "I can hear the crowds; they're yelling at this man…to put the crown of thorns on him because he says he's a king. He's King of the Jews. Romans are law here."

"How does it feel to be a Roman soldier, a Centurian?" I asked.

"Whooh! A lot of pride! We are the superior race!" she exclaimed.

"Does your physical body feel anything now?" I had her check in.

Heather observed some interesting aspects, "I feel bigger, stronger. I feel like I'm in Heather's body. I feel the clothing...the boots, helmet, the skirt, you know, of the soldier."

"Does it feel comfortable?" I wondered

"Oh yeah, I'm okay. Heather feels guilty, you know, 'cause this is Jesus we've done this to," she explained as she began to show some physical discomfort with the remorse.

I reassured her, "Don't worry about that right now. Relax."

"He was an upstart at that time. There was only one King. That was Ceasar!" she commented. "He's so calm and all. He says he forgives us for what we do."

I reminded Heather that it was fine to observe these scenes. Apparently, they flashed vividly, as well as rapidly before her. Several minutes passed before she spoke again. "Before I let go and gave myself permission to move on, I was on the northern frontier of the Roman Empire battling with the barbarian hordes. Their bodies are lying all around. I was proud to kill for the Roman Empire." She frowned and grimaced as the next scenes moved through. "I've got a sword pressed to the knee, the left knee and then through the chest on my right side. I died then, but I see an awful lot of other wounds too."

More time elapsed until she moved on, "Now I'm in Scotland again, overseeing the people, wearing the kilt because I'm trying to blend in. I'm still a soldier, part of the Roman contingency left there to keep peace. I'm just enjoying the peace and the Highlands."

"Relax. See if there's anything else important that you need to know regarding that time," I suggested.

"Doesn't seem to be much else there," she responded. Then gradually, the energy changed. "I feel like I'm shivering. I am shivering! I don't feel cold; it's James' anger, his excitement!"

"What's it all about?" I asked.

"James just joined up; he has a new uniform! His anger is about John Brown, being at his trial," she said. "Anger again at an outsider coming in and trying to tell us how we can live. Then more anger and news of Charleston and northerners are coming in and interfering in the happiness that Virginians have, siding with the Confederacy...all the excitement of joining up!"

She paused a bit to consider all the information she was receiving. "I can tell that James became friends with JEB Stuart during that John Brown incident and that Stuart knows James well because of the friendship. He knows that James is part mountain goat and so is his horse. He knows these mountains like the back of his hand. James is good at maps and scouting the terrain. If he goes someplace once, you know he can take someone back to that area. So, he's being used primarily as a scout, but for official purposes. He can be found in Berkley County, Co. B of 1st Virginia. James trained and mustered with them and fought with them when he could return from scouting duties in time to form in.

"There's a lot of envy from the other soldiers toward James. He has to work harder to earn their trust and their respect, to show that he's a good warrior, not just a scout...you know, that he can hold his own in both places. Even though he's a 'loner,' when called on to fall in with the company, then he's very much a 'team player.' He can follow orders even though his temper does tend to get him in trouble." Heather enjoyed a lot of laughter here as she recalled some of those instances. "He's headstrong with a bad temper...very straightforward and doesn't mind telling his superiors what he thinks they should do, even though he's a lowly private and will stay that way.

"James 'colored' for them at the Stone Bridge area right before the battle in the Manassas area. There'd been some skirmishing and stuff but no big battle yet," she commented. "He's waiting to be called into action and is waiting to follow Stuart out." Her breathing became more rapid while the scenes became more explicit.

"They kept yelling at me! I got tired of hearing that name ...not quite so temperamental ...with the horse. It's so much simpler if I'm ridin' the trail, scouting by myself instead of ridin' by twos, by fours. Right face, left face!" Heather exclaimed. "You've got a horse in front of you, a horse right beside you," she laughed at her own exasperation. "It's not easy. It's much easier doing it alone. Ole' Virginia...I'll do anything for Virginia.

"Yes, I couldn't get it right. I know how James feels...all that anger," she observed. "Why don't they stop yelling at me! I get it, I get it," Heather laughed. "Just stop yelling. There's so many similarities between both lives, same emotions too."

We watched patiently to see what would occur next, if anything. Suddenly, James is again describing the battle, "Well I'm back at

Manassas now. We just whipped those boys in blue and boy are they skedaddling!. We want to chase 'em. We wanna go all the way to Washington 'cause we're still fresh. But, the generals are saying "no," that we've got to fall back." James truly sounded disappointed.

"He's got gutts!" Heather observed. "Some of 'em do. James stole a Yankee uniform off one of the dead…waited 'til they got close to their ranks, left his horse, changed into the Yankee blue. He's walking around their camps, listening to their conversations."

"That's pretty brave," I commented. "Where's all this?"

"This was up around the Washington area, on the Potomac River after the withdrawal from Manassas. He suddenly has a Spanish accent; he doesn't have a Virginia accent He can blend in and listen, then report back to Stuart. James is just walking around and blending in, bold as day as if he's one of 'em."

At this point, I wanted her to check in for any physical sensations. She replied, "Relaxed! There's some tingling in my fingers and my left knee. I'm aware of James' spirits…right now he's in very good spirits! He's still in that Yankee camp, just very cocky, like 'hey look at me!' Well, don't look at me, but you know how he is. I'm really blending with the scenery. I'm a really good scout and spy. I have to say he's got gutts!

"I want to see a mountain area," she continued. "There's a battle there. The reason I kind of laughed about saying 'going back to that area' is because I haven't been to that area in this lifetime. I don't know what James was doing there, but he was spying in that place too and around the town. There was a battle too."

"You started to mention your left knee," I interjected.

"Yes! It's vibrating somehow. It feels like, not a tingling now, but a vibration!" Heather exclaimed. "It's different from the tingling, stronger. My hands are a bit tingly. I noticed with each image that I processed with the knee, I was either doing something with my hands or I had a weapon in my hands, or my hands were tied. I've had a lot of reinjuries from the rib cage, from the right side, and I have arthritis there now. At one point when I was processing the images it felt almost like a branch hitting me behind the knees. It was sharp enough that I processed that and it disappeared. I'm very comfortable now, no pain anywhere.

"I've been a warrior many times…from a fox hole in World War I and II to Valley Forge to Rome to…but I especially like my mountains," she trailed off as this session came to a close.

Buchanan Castle

The original lands of Buchanan were awarded to Anselan by Malcom II for his services against the Danes. His descendants later assumed the surname of Buchanan. After 600 years on Loch Lomonside, the Buchanans lost these lands in 1682. The lands were then acquired by the 3rd Marquis, Duke of Montrose, a member of the Graham family.

Buchanan Castle burned down between 1850 and Christmas of 1852. By 1854 a huge baronial mansion was built in its place. In 1941 Rudolf Hess who was Hitler's deputy was imprisoned in the Buchanan House.

The ruins still standing are quite impressive and reputedly haunted. For the stout of heart, many people muster up the courage to comb Buchanan's somber hallways.

Buchanan House (castle) as it stands today. It's overgrown halls are inhabited by active spirits.

Gettysburg

All around the breakfast table Sunday morning July 6, 1997 the guests of the inn exchanged cordialities. We were privileged to stay overnight in an establishment in the midst of the Gettysburg Battlefield. Finally, one brave individual broke the ice on another topic. "I was sitting on the terrace after dark last night," he began. "Behind me I could hear footsteps of a large man wearing boots, walking on a wooden plank walkway. From that same direction I also heard noises like a rifle being shifted from shoulder to shoulder," the guest looked around the table to see how the others were reacting. So far, no one laughed. Each face showed genuine interest. "I got up from my chair, but saw no one there. All I saw were trees and the railroad tracks below the bank".

Several people nodded their heads in agreement. "Yeh, there're some pretty strange things reported consistently around Gettysburg," one reenactor reminded them. "Friday evening I was standing across the road, looking into Forney's field in the direction of the Peace Light. There didn't seem to be any people out; but a real filmy haze floated through the field," the Tennessee man observed. "The next thing I witnessed were little bursts of light sputtering intermittently throughout the field. At first they reminded me of lightning bugs, only larger and quicker. I also observed that there weren't any lightning bugs out, nor could I have seen them through that fog. It truly seemed like the smoke of battle."

Various visitors chimed in with accounts of experiences on that battlefield. Apparently, everyone present was a frequent Gettysburg visitor. Richard who reenacts with the 7th Tennessee Infantry was walking across Forney's field at dusk one July evening in 1993. "The four of us were in Confederate uniforms, moving slowly and quietly through that area where so many Rebs had been mowed down. I felt like somebody was following us. Two of our guys glanced over their shoulders and saw three Confederates walking directly behind us. They'd just appeared out of nowhere! One of them commented to us, 'You're all here now; it's okay. We can go.' And they did! The five of us watched the three disappear!"

Early on the morning of July 2, 1863 Colonel Patrick Kelly led the remaining men of the Irish Brigade into Union lines. The total strength of the unit had been reduced to the 63rd, 69th and 88th New York's 240 men and the 28th Massachusetts's 224 and 66 soldiers of the 116th Pennsylvania Volunteers. Under Mulholland's command, the force was posted on Cemetery Ridge near Plum Run.

From this position they watched Hood and McLaw's Rebel divisions launch their attack against Sickles' Third Corps who'd advanced into Devil's Den, the Wheatfield and the Peach Orchard. Late that afternoon, the Irish were called to arms.

Chaplain of the 88th NY, Father Corby climbed atop a boulder so that he could be seen and heard by hundreds of men. He offered them absolution for their sins before doing battle. Cradling muskets in one hand and holding their cap in the other, the Sons of Erin knelt on one knee and bowed their heads. Each man humbled himself before the Great Creator. Corby reminded them that none would receive a Christian burial if they deserted their flag and their noble cause.

Corporal of the 12th Virginia Cavalry, Co. A Frank Belluardo found himself touring the Gettysburg Battlefield, Spring of 1993. He and a buddy, both dressed in Confederate gray, entered the Devil's Den parking area. Frank wandered over to the Slaughter Pen and perched on a rock. His buddy walked up the drive toward the stream in the woods beyond.

What happened to Frank after that was more than startling. "All sounds of nature ceased. The voices of the few tourists above Devil's Den became muffled and distant," he explains. "The hair on my head raised; something about the situation felt weird yet familiar! I was sure someone or something was there," Frank continues. "I experienced this odd compulsion to look over my shoulder. Still, I managed to resist it as though a state of dread." Meanwhile, Frank's companion continued to talk to him from a distance, not noticing anything special.

The Corporal felt an icy chill run up his back. "I looked down at my chest. There was a bayonet sticking through me from back to front!"

Behind him stood an excited Federal soldier. The guy appeared to be in his mid-to-late twenties, hardened in the face, but not old. He was clean-shaven but scruffy in appearance and had dark hair. "I finally got one...finally got one! I finally got a Reb! It's okay now; everything's okay."

Frank shakily asked him what he meant. The absence of pain hadn't dawned on him yet.

"I'm free!" the blue-coat was elated. "I'm free! I can go now; I'm finally free. Thank you." Then he faded away, the bayonet disappearing with him.

Frank was stunned. He asked his friend who was approaching, "Did you feel or hear anything over this way?"

"No, it was noticeably quiet. I heard you speak to someone," his companion commented.

Of the Confederates present in 1863, Frank probably represented to the Yank one of Robertson's Texas boys or one of McLaw's Alabamians. Whether the phantom was a Celtic soul of the Irish or one of Sickles' men, we may never know. What is certain is that one Union soldier was released that day into Heaven.

Frank Belluardo is presently Commander of the Blue Mountain Boys Cavalry in Tennessee. He is also a member of Clan Stevenson of Scotland and has done extensive research on his clan. They were most assuredly among those fighting with William Wallace in the Wars of Independence.

Experiences of 'the other plane' are not foreign to Frank. In March, 1995 he was present in Birmingham, Alabama for the 1st Annual Reenactment of the Battle of Bridgeport. Activities were set on the extreme right of the original theater of fighting. About 3:00 A.M. he was wakened by noises, but couldn't see anything from his tent flap. He decided that it was probably the horses moving about camp. He returned to his slumber.

"Soon, I was startled awake again," he says. "Camp sounds surrounded me—metal clanking, muffled verbal orders being given, bayonets being socketed, people hollering, 'Get in line; form up!'" These activities continued for fifteen minutes. Frank thought he was late rising, so he began dressing. "It was 5:00 A.M.—barely getting light. I got outside my tent and nobody was there! The camp was empty. "I talked to a few other men about it. They'd heard it too, but had decided it was too early for them to get up."

July 5, 1997 the 10th Louisiana Infantry from Ontario, Canada visited Gettysburg. Tom Brooks of that unit took this photo of his two buddies, Steve Mayes and Mike Christianson. The men were crossing the Triangular Field about 7:30 P.M.; the visibility was clear. Tom stopped to take this photo and captured more on film than he expected. Of 24 negatives on the roll of film, this one was cloudy and nearly white.

A Familiar Face

A friend of Marguerite's had sent her a copy of *Echoes of Valor* and *A Thundering Silence*, well aware that Marguerite had a very special connection to Gettysburg. One or more of the energies associated with Gettysburg were attracted to her and manifested at will, not only in that town but others as well.

Marguerite traveled to Charlottesville to meet with me. And, I looked forward to spending some time with this woman who obviously had a strong 'unexplainable' attraction to Gettysburg, as so many people do.

She sat in my living room and began to describe her visits, "I've been to Gettysburg at least five times this year. I can't get enough of it." Then Marguerite began to recount a recent trip, "My friend Janine went over with me in March. We decided to take our Prayer Books with us. Janine felt that a prayer service would help some of the remaining spirits. We wished to lend them some peace."

I nodded in agreement, "That's a wonderful idea! What happened?"

Marguerite continued, "As soon as we arrived, we went down Confederate Avenue in the vicinity of the North Carolina Monument. The trip previous to this I had seen a shadowy figure in that area. That's why we chose that spot to visit first. There were hardly any people around at all. We put a blanket down and began an evening prayer," she said. "Soon that soundless vacuum came—no sounds of nature, no cars, nothing. Instantly, we heard footsteps in the dry grass approaching us from behind. Janine continued reading; then I read aloud too. As the prayer was completed, we looked around to see who'd joined us. No one was in sight."

Next, Marguerite told me of another incredible visit she made with her friend Anne in 1993. "Anne drove into the parking lot of the inn after dinner. As soon as we drove past the front porch, Anne spotted an officer sitting in the rocking chair. She said, 'Please look over there and tell me what you see.'" Marguerite vividly remembered the evening. "I didn't understand what she meant at first. So, she repeated it. 'Look on the porch! Describe to me what's there!' Anne had been adamant."

"I did all right," Marguerite filled in the remaining details. "Geez—was I startled. There he sat in a Confederate-gray uniform, a grin on his face, twinkle in his eye and smoking a cigar. 'Thank heavens you see him too,' was Anne's remark. She thought she was really 'going over the edge.'"

Marguerite explained further, "He's quite a prankster. He even held up his cigar to make sure I noticed it. The night before that he'd been in our room smoking a cigar. I had yelled at him to take the cigar outside. I demanded that he get out with it. There was so much smoke in our room that it bothered my allergies."

"By the time we walked to the porch that second evening," she continued, "he'd disappeared but the smoke lingered. What really 'put the icing on the cake' was that face! I knew it from somewhere. Yet, I couldn't put a name with it."

Marguerite still gets chills from the final recognition. I asked her, "How did you figure it out?"

"It took a few weeks," she explained. "First I looked at my family pictures. The officer reminded me of an uncle. But there was some stronger resemblance I couldn't quite put my finger on. A book in the library with Confederate officers' pictures gave me my answer. That guy on the porch was the 'spitting image' of Brigadier General Richard Garnett, killed at Gettysburg. His body was never found afterward."

She talked more about his travels. "He will come to my bedroom in Pennsylvania, or he'll visit me here. It doesn't matter where I am. He finds me. He always knows where I am. He provides me with a very protective feeling, almost 'looked after'. I've never felt threatened by him," she explained.

I then described how simple it was for the spirits to manifest so effortlessly and to travel at will. "They are not always confined to a material location as so many people believe. Do you recall any energy drains or physical effects from this entity around you?" I inquired of Marguerite.

She considered this carefully before answering. "Only one time when I and a compadre were traveling to Gettysburg did I notice that. The town was busy, so we were able to get only one bed to share. My friend was recovering from recent surgery. That night in Gettysburg I was restless - absolutely could not sleep. I chose not to disturb my companion, so I rose from bed with the intention of going downstairs. When I started toward the door, I felt this strong presence between me and the door! He wouldn't let me out of the room . At that point that's all I can remember. It was as though I was anesthetized. I immediately fell asleep very deeply until the next day," Marguerite replied.

Through the time of our meeting, I learned much about Marguerite. While still married she and her husband began reenacting with a Civil War unit. At that time it seemed that the Civil War was the only interest they had in common. As the marriage dissolved, so did Marguerite's reenacting career. The Living History programs at Eckley Miner's Museum in Pennsylvania, however, continue to draw her for participation. St. James Episcopal Church, built in the 1860's, is her favorite station. It is there that she is most comfortable. Yet, the incredible fascination she has for Gettysburg is ever stronger.

"When I go to Gettysburg, I have to walk and look and feel the place," Marguerite explained. "I don't know what I'm looking for, but I have to go as often as I can. The uncanny events started in 1987. The activities were quite prevalent in 1988 and have never entirely ceased. In 1993 I noticed lots of stronger energy, but 1994 hadn't changed either," she commented.

"Can you recall how you first became aware of these presences?" I wondered.

Marguerite's eyes lit up. "You bet I can! The first encounter was while I was sleeping one night in Gettysburg. I heard a soft sound which seemed like my robe falling off the bed. It made barely enough noise to wake me. Immediately I realized that someone was either sitting down on or getting up from my bed. I was in a daze! It didn't seem real!" she exclaimed. "Normally I wear several pieces of silver jewelry. This night I had worn it to bed, and I was lying on my right side. I felt an extreme coldness come up across the bed towards my face. Next, there was a soft touch on my left wrist and my cheek. 'Am I dreaming?' I wondered. What followed was the slight odor of cigar smoke filling my room. Suddenly, I realized that it was leaving. I sat up and began to cry. I said, 'No, don't go!' It departed anyway. I sat there in awe of the whole experience, and eventually I fell back asleep.

"My favorite place of all at Gettysburg is the Peace Light," Marguerite went on with the story. "That following morning quite early, I rose quietly so not to disturb my daughter and mother who had accompanied me. As I arrived at the Peace Light, it was daylight. I checked my watch for the time. The watch band and bracelets on my left arm were completely tarnished! These pieces had never tarnished before," she emphasized. "Shortly afterward I returned to my room, heading straight to the bathroom. As I gazed into the mirror, I saw that my left earring was tarnished too! The right one was fine. I am convinced that the touch on my arm the previous night had something to do with these pieces discoloring," Marguerite said.

I was intrigued by her experiences, particularly how consistent they were. The details of the tarnished items were also consistent with two other stories of belt buckles worn by reenactors on the battlefields mysteriously becoming discolored.

She was happy to continue. "Another trip to the Peace Light late one evening was startling. My daughter Marie sat there with me a brief time. No one else was in sight. Suddenly, everything became unnaturally quiet, like a vacuum, not one sound. I thought, 'it's never this quiet here; what's happening?' Then I heard the penetrating moan of a man in ungodly pain! That man was in terrible agony by the sound of it. I took Marie's hand and led her away. 'We should go now!' was all I could say to her," Marguerite described.

"One evening of yet another excursion to Gettysburg, Janine and myself were sitting in the bar of the inn where we had chosen to stay. We had just returned from dinner. Since I wasn't feeling well that evening, I bought honey and blackberry brandy to put in my hot tea," Marguerite recalled. "There was a man staying at the inn whom I'd become interested in. He was with us in the bar that evening. I offered him some brandy. He was quite agreeable to that but wished to go upstairs and check on his elderly father first. While he did so, I went to my room to fetch the brandy," she explained.

"Long after I returned with the brandy, Janine and I were still waiting for the gentleman to come back," Marguerite expressed her disappointment. "Janine continued reading; then terrible banging and slamming noises started around the inn. 'Is that the wind causing that?' I asked her. 'Oh yeah, right! was her sarcastic reply."

"You don't think so, huh?" Marguerite wondered. "Well, I sat there a bit longer. I finally mentioned to Janine that I might go up and knock on my new friend's door to see what was delaying him.

Marguerite relived the chills from the experience. "Out of thin air, I was grabbed firmly by the wrist. It was a hot sensation, as if by anger!" she said. "The thought of this invisible person holding me there startled me. Needless to say, I didn't go check on my friend.

"Janine wasn't ready to go up for bed, but I was," Marguerite said. "I drained my teacup and headed toward the stairs. 'I've got news for you girl. You're in trouble!' Janine told me.

"Not knowing what I would find, I ascended the stairs alone. As soon as I opened the door, I saw the mess. My bed was strewn apart as though someone had wrestled in it!" Marguerite exclaimed. "That bed was perfectly in order when I left it earlier."

It would seem that she had acquired an unusual, possessive admirer. The evidence to substantiate this idea was overwhelming. "I've come to recognize his presence well," she explained. "He knows my name and has called it in the middle of the night at various locations. Sometimes he will sit at the foot of my bed and watch me sleep," Marguerite declared.

She remembered another example of her phantom's effect on her life. "I had met another man whom I planned to meet in Gettysburg. Something bizarre came up at work to prevent me from going on the trip. I was terribly angry and disappointed," Marguerite recalled. "Yet that night at home, a male spirit manifested in my bedroom. The experience was as if to show me that I didn't have to go to Gettysburg.

He could travel to see me. But the entire sequence of events was so noticeable because it was a date whom I had planned to spend time with. It was the only instance that I was prevented from going there."

I wondered, with the number of encounters she had witnessed, if there was any other physical evidence of movement or activities. "Most of these spirits retain the characteristics (ego) of the person whom they once were in this dimension," I explained to her. "Have you seen or know of any personal objects being moved when you felt a spirit's presence?"

"Sure I have!" she knew exactly where this was leading. "I used to own an exquisite Victorian perfume vial. The fragrance I kept in it was originally from the 1800,s, but I can't find it in the stores anymore. Both the bottle and the scent were my favorites," she said. "Also at the time, I wore a thin silver band on my thumb. It was plain but delicate, similar to a wedding band. One night in Gettysburg I placed both items together on the night stand as I went to bed."

"When I rose the next morning, the ring and vial were missing." Marguerite described the scene further, "I looked all over that room. The bed was on a solid platform, so the items hadn't fallen under that. I even retrieved my flashlight from my car and searched the room again. They simply disappeared in the night. They've never shown up since."

I agreed with her on their pranks. "Often the items which the spirits move or take away are those which they feel a personal attachment to. Or, they will affect the items which we have a personal attachment to in order to assuredly get our attention. What other observances have you made?" I asked her.

"One night I was asleep in my room. My contact lenses were on the dresser, as were my glasses. Consequently, I couldn't see well when I woke up. A man's voice was calling my name. I sat bolt upright in bed. There was a flash of light near the chair. Then it was gone," Marguerite said. "You see, when he visits he likes to sit in a chair. There'll be times at home when he shows up as a shadowy form at night. He'll stand near my bed, or sit in a chair, and watch me sleep. Eventually he does something slight but distinct enough to wake me. I know also he has traveled with me to friends' homes in other towns.

"Marie accompanied me another time when we rented a room

with no chair in it. That particular night in Gettysburg I was awakened as an incredible coldness entered the room. He sat at the foot of my bed. The impression on the bed was so strong that the springs moved with his weight. The only thing between us was the blanket! The electricity was phenomenal. This freezing chill began in my feet, traveled up my right leg, and into my hip!" she declared. "I didn't know what to do. Suddenly he was gone. I was sorry that I didn't turn to look at him."

Marguerite continued with the account. "During that same trip, I set my alarm clock three different nights in order to rise early for a visit to the Peace Light. Each night it was turned off as we slept. I thought I was going crazy! But Marie assured me that she saw me set it each night.

"Marie was taking a shower but kept the bathroom door open. Through the clear plastic shower curtain, she saw a male figure dressed in gray uniform walk past the door three times," Marguerite added to the details of the same excursion. "What I had not mentioned to Marie previously was that I saw the same figure outside on the battlefield earlier that day. The gray-clad soldier was so distinct that I could make out the rifle barrel and ramrod. Yet his face was hidden by the tree leaves."

Considering all of Marguerite's experiences, I asked for her final comments on them.

"None of this is a bad feeling. I have no fear of him in any way. Normally if I am upset, restless, or unwell, he will come to ease my discomfort," she responded to my words. "But this very last trip to Gettysburg, I had pneumonia and didn't realize it. I was feeling lousy. It was the only time he had not appeared to ease my mind. I even said to Janine, 'I want to see him. I can't understand where he is this time!'" Marguerite described her reactions.

Then she turned to me and said, "As far as saying good-bye to him,' I can't say that I want to."

Gettysburg's Horses

The value of horses during the Civil War was of the utmost importance not just as a cavalry mount but as transportation for the caissons and limbers of the artillery, the supply wagons and the ambulances. Because of the mortality rate and general scarcity of horses compared to men and ammunition, the farmers resorted to many desperate, creative lengths to hide and keep their equine stock. Current estimates of horses killed during the American Civil War are near one-and-a half million. At Gettysburg's battle alone, there were 72,243 horses, approximately 5,000 of which were killed in those three days.

Joshua Chamberlain rode on Charlamayne. J.E.B. Stuart was there with three mounts-Virginia, My Maryland, and Highfly. Robert E. Lee brought Traveller and his other favorite Lucy Long. All of these survived, but so many were less fortunate. Landowners and residents found their properties littered with carcasses of horses during and after the Battle of Gettysburg. One woman returned home finding seventeen dead horses on her land, several of which had to be set on fire to dispose of them. The stench of burning hair and rotting horseflesh was overwhelming for days. Orchards were spoiled for the season from rotting carcasses and wells were tainted to the point of being unusable.

The desperately needed animals were used and abused in other manners too. Properly shoeing them as the war progressed was nearly unheard of. Consequently, many of the creatures' hooves were worn off to the quick, and were abandoned because of severe hoof-sores. Even more wretched sights and sounds though were the horses which had been shot but not mortally so. The poor creatures walked around groaning and neighing in pain and confusion. Eventually, someone came along and shot them to put them out of further misery.

For Steve Bennett and his four reenactor pals, then of the 10th Alabama Regiment, these statistics were far from their minds as they drove late at night up to the entrance of the Gettysburg National Cemetery. It was July, 1993 the 130th Anniversary of the Battle of Gettysburg when this strange circumstance took place.

Two of the men, Steve included, emerged from their vehicle and walked around near it. Immediately, they were approached by a group of several horses, various colors, fully tacked and ready to be ridden into action. The men assumed that they belonged to the other reenactors and had possibly gotten loose. Steve and his companion walked even closer to get a good look. There was no doubt but what they were real horses. 'Yet why were they completely accoutred so late at night?' Steve wondered. The men hastened a departure before the horses' owners reappeared.

As the soldiers drove toward camp, a pair of park police waived them down. Steve rolled the window down to hear why they were being stopped. "Hey, can you men tell us exactly where the Confederate camp is? We need to get to the Commander General's tent," one officer explained.

Steve and his friends responded with directions. Then the next question posed by the police nearly cornered the reenactors. "Do you know if all the Confederate horses are accounted for? Some of the folks here in town called us, complaining that a herd of horses were running loose through town. We just came from the Union side, and all their cavalry is tied up for the night."

The Rebs kept silent about their experience in the cemetery. They continued on their journey back to camp but with a rather uneasy feeling. It was confirmed the following day that no Confederate cavalry, had been missing the night before. Steve and his friends couldn't resist temptation. They returned to the National Cemetery. In the light of day, the men discovered the marked location of forty or more horses killed at Gettysburg in 1863. Realization set in; what they had encountered the previous night were spirits of so many of these fallen animals.

As the movie "Gettysburg" was being filmed, Steve Bennett was present as one of the five-thousand reenactors used as supporting actors. He recalls one Union soldier's experience around the grounds of the filming, eight miles from the original battlefield. The Yankee had risen early one morning to the sight and sound of a colorful bagpiper crossing the misty field toward him. As soon as another person joined him, the mysterious piper vanished. Could this vision have come from one of the Iron Brigade's Celts?

Metaphysical occurrences are not unusual for Steve. While a youth of 13 years, he lived in Germany with his family. Steve's favorite hobby was collecting Nazi German helmets, jackets with bullet holes, including other articles left over from World War II. To borrow a Japanese term, Steve had frequent "mind-hauntings" of seven German soldiers attached to these collected articles. Another notable aspect of his life was that his bedroom always seemed to be icy cold compared to any other rooms in the Bennett home. The youth was prone to catch frequent colds and various sickness.

His mother often came into his room trying to convince him of the importance of cleaning it up. This was a frequent occasion until the day when she had a similar vision to her son's. Mrs. Bennett walked into Steve's bedroom alone one morning after he'd departed for school. Staggered all around his room were the images of seven soldiers from World War II.

This startling experience really "iced the cake" for Steve's mother. She would no longer enter his room, but all the German war memorabilia had to go. Afterward, his room became warm, comparable to the rest of the house, and many of his illnesses tapered off.

Even today in his home in Fredericksburg, Steve is reminded of "other levels of existence." Winter of 1997, the great grandson of the Japanese Commander of forces in Iwojima stayed with Steve and his wife. This young man collected military artifacts also, and made some such purchases during his visit to Fredericksburg. One sword of this selection particularly caught the young man's attention.

That night he chose to sleep with the sword next to him. What resulted was a "mind-haunting" similar to Steve's as a boy. The Japanese gentleman dreamed vividly of several individuals who'd been killed by the use of this sword.

Elmira Prison

The last day of fighting at Gettysburg July 3, 1863 , General Lee ordered a major assault on Cemetery Ridge. The Confederate troops led by Ewell were driven off Culp's Hill, too early to support the main assault. It remained for JEB Stuart's weary troops who'd just arrived late the previous day to attack around the Union right.

Stuart's thrust was stopped by the cavalrymen of Brigadier General Gregg after intense thundering mounted charges across Rummel farm. Meanwhile, Confederate batteries fired two hours of charges to pave the way for the main assault on part of Cemetery Ridge. Then twelve thousand Confederates led by General Pickett trudged bravely across the open fields toward the Union Second Corps. The small copse of trees ahead of them would later be named 'the Angle'.

By the time they crossed the Emmitsburg Road, Union canister and rifle fire had decimated their formations. Pickett lost most of his men in that charge, but a few were driven back and more were captured.

A drenching summer rain pelted Lee's men on the evening of July 4th as they began their slow, sloggy journey back toward the Potomac. Four-thousand Confederates, however, were headed in the opposite direction.

When the Evans family purchased their home in Elmira thirty-five years ago, the fate of Confederate prisoners of 1863 was not a consideration. The house would sit empty for twenty-five years before the Evanses and their two sons moved into it.

Mike occupied the back, upstairs bedroom, while his brother Todd claimed the front bedroom. One smaller room remained in between the two. Life in the large house began quite smoothly. But, that circumstance changed as soon as the first week of July arrived.

The two men were sound asleep in their rooms. In the wee hours of the morning, both were awakened by an incredibly loud, fearsome noise outside their rooms. Both ran out into the hall, very upset. Neither could identify the sounds which had ceased as soon as they met in the hall.

The remainder of the night was uneventful. But, the next morning at breakfast, Todd was noticeably agitated. Mike attempted a discussion regarding the night's disturbances. Todd would have no part of it "Something happened! Something happened up there!" was his only comment before jumping up from the table and leaving the room.

Another year passed calmly. Then again in early July at 2:00 a.m., Mike was awakened by the sound of heavy footsteps, slowly ascending the stairs just outside his locked bedroom. Then it entered Mike's room and pinned him flat onto the bed! Mike couldn't breathe! It was as though he was being suffocated by his invisible attacker. In the midst of his panic, Mike was sweating like mad. He frantically prayed for help, and it came. Still, it took all the physical strength he had to barely raise his arm to turn on the lamp beside his bed.

Suddenly, the struggle ended, and Mike was able to sit up. He walked across the room, then turned the overhead light on. Nothing! Except for himself, the bedroom was empty. He traipsed downstairs, checking on things there. All was well. There were absolutely no indications of an intruder. He retraced his steps upstairs, returning to the scene of his attack.

"All right! Come and get me!" Mike yelled angrily in a challenge. Still...nothing. He left his door open the remainder of the evening and went back to sleep.

The following morning over breakfast, Mike described for Todd everything that had happened the previous night. His brother sat there quietly listening, taking it all in. When he spoke Todd assured Mike that he was familiar with the experience. "Remember that night a year ago when we both ran out in the hall?"

Mike nodded his head, "Sure! Who could forget?"

Todd who is 6'1" tall, weighing 225 lbs. and a serious weight-lifter had had the same attacker as Mike. "Only I saw the guy!" Mike exclaimed. "I saw a large grey figure in a grey coat and a slouch hat like a Civil War soldier. He had me flattened out on the bed so that I couldn't move!"

Other activities continued in that small room between the two occupied bedrooms. It is essentially empty except for a few small furniture items. One occasion between 3:00 and 4:00 a.m., both men heard someone thumping and bumping around in the spare room. Mike listened carefully to the sounds of fingers strumming on an object. The next day during daylight hours, he entered the room and spotted an area fan. As Mike strummed his fingers across the protective wire, he recognized it as the same sound.

When their dad was still living, he would hear things in the house which were unaccounted for. Mike and his father sat in the living room downstairs one morning. A heavy ball could be heard rolling around in the upstairs hallway. His dad smiled, "Who's up there?"

"Nobody. There's only you and I here," Mike replied. At this his dad insisted that his son go check. Mike declined to go upstairs.

His dad smiled again, "Well, I guess we just heard a squirrel."

Since these earlier days, Mike has moved out of the Evans house, but Todd remains there with his mother. Todd sleeps in the back bedroom, as so much of the psychic activity seems to be focused in the front one. He keeps the door to that one closed at all times. From time-to-time Todd reminds the entity that the front room is its as long as it doesn't bother him. Most of the time this approach works, but once in a while Todd still finds that the door to the front bedroom has been opened during the night hours.

Again in September of 1997, Todd was awakened at 5:00 a.m. in his back bedroom. Someone was bending over his face and breathing very heavily like a real heavy 'sigh.' Todd sat up and turned the lamp on. It was audible again with the light on. For some reason Todd moved the dresser slightly to one side. The noise stopped; then he heard it again.

As events progressed through the years in which the Evanses have lived there, Mike and Todd did some investigating. The house is situated on what was a section of Elmira Prison. The back bedroom overlooks the river which ran through the camp. Even though the house had not been built at that time, it is old enough that some of its timbers may have come from part of the prison.

Those 4,000 Confederates captured at the Angle at Gettysburg were sent to Elmira Prison those same early days in July, 1863.

Plymouth Retreat

There was a period of several years when Ken Bucher of Fort Branch Supply, portrayed a Confederate sharp shooter. During those days when he still carried a gun, the reenactment of the Battle of Plymouth, North Carolina of 1863 was one which vividly affected the sutler's life.

Ken recalls his experience as the movie company asked him to play the role in their documentary filmed in 1992. "These sharp shooters were men chosen for bravery and courage under fire. This Confederate soldier was no exception; he held off the whole Union Army while the Confederate troops retreated from the town of Plymouth."

The original house, complete with bullet holes and bullets from that engagement, remains intact and occupied. Ken agreed to characterize the soldier, but was completely unaware of the details surrounding his death. He approached the front door and continues to describe the events. "As soon as I arrived, I began feeling funny. Here I am in uniform, with a Whitworth, an old Confederate sharp shooter's rifle. Suddenly, I found myself doing stupid things which I normally would not have done."

The woman who lived in the house greeted Ken at the door. A very genteel, southern elderly lady welcomed him into her living room. He entered and greeted her, "I took off my hat and dipped way down low. Next, I grabbed her hand then kissed it. Suddenly, I realized what I was doing," Ken explains. "I asked myself at the time 'what am I doing? This isn't me. I don't do this kind of stuff!' I was quite gracious."

141

His own genteel manners simply 'melted' the woman. But for Ken a gnawing feeling was growing, a peculiar sensation in his stomach. The woman matter of factly stated, "Well, I suppose you want to go up to the room."

He replied, "Yeah, I guess I should." As Ken walked up the long staircase, he became aware of the television crew preparing to film the sequence. "The farther up those stairs I went, I became more scared. It was the feeling you get when you almost have a car wreck, an anxiety attack." He progressed upward continuing to have stronger sensations of panic. "I opened the door into that room; it was like 'BAM' "! he exclaims. "I had goose bumps; I began shaking. I was scared! Yet, I wasn't as much so as I was going to be," Ken says.

As he sat in a chair waiting for the production people to get underway, the cameraman said, "Do you want to go ahead and set up?"

"Where's the window that he shot out of?" Ken asked for direction.

The man pointed and said, "This window here."

Ken approached it and opened it wide. "Once I opened that window, I began to shiver. I went ice cold and was really shaking then," he declares. Then he turned around, looking at the cameraman.

"Are you alright?" the guy asked Ken.

"Yeah I'm okay," he responded hesitantly. "But I'm pretty shakey."

"Are you sick or what's wrong?" the cameraman was genuinely concerned. "You look a little pale."

"No, I'm fine in that respect, but I sure feel really funny," Ken said.

Meanwhile, the director turned to the cameraman, "Don't take that camera off of him." Everything that occurred in the room was captured on film. Ken paced the floor in anticipation.

"Here they come," the director announced.

The sharp shooter went into action. Ken kneeled down and loaded his Whitworth. "Once I stuck that gun out the window, my hands started vibrating, "he recalls the exact sensations. "I was scared, nervous. I turned to look straight toward the camera."

"You're as white as a sheet!" the cameraman exclaimed.

"I'm scared!" Ken explained.

"What're scared of?" he asked.

All Ken could say was that he was 'scared.' "So, I fired the first shot and the nervousness was entirely gone. It was suddenly all business. I was just killing Yankees," he says. "But I was still like ice. I vividly recall one episode with a Yankee outside who I supposedly shot. He took a really hard hit and fell. It was so realistic that it didn't seem to be reenacted at all."

The prearranged scenario was set up so that Ken would fire four rounds. Then he was supposed to die. "Well, I fired that fourth one. Then I took my hit, falling backwards on the floor. I was lying there a while and they're still filming me."

The elderly woman had quietly mounted the stairs while the action took place. But as she approached the scene, she clasped her hands to her face, "Oh my heavens! He's lying there exactly where he died!"

Suddenly, Ken was up like a cat. "I wasn't going to lie there any longer than I had to. Now, I recall that once I began firing, my color returned."

In the original event of the retreat from Plymouth, there was an officer in the room with the sharp shooter. He commanded the Reb to leave, but the soldier refused. The officer left, giving up on the determined soldier. He was finally hit as a cannon full of grapeshot from the riverbed was fired upon him. He fell backward away from his window. Yet, he didn't expire there immediately. The Reb pulled himself up sufficiently to drag himself to those stairs. As soon as he reached the banister, he fell the entire distance downstairs where he died.

The sharp shooter's body, riddled with grapeshot left a massive trail of blood as he traveled from the window to the first floor of the house. As hard as they tried to clean it, the occupants could not remove the bloodstains. Eventually, the wooden floor had to be replaced.

Four years after this portrayal, Ken summarizes his feelings. "After it was over, it was still such a powerful experience! That sharp shooter was with me. I bonded with him. I've characterized that same person since then at the same place too, but none of those events were nearly as spectacular as the first."

Return

Noisy geese honked as they skimmed across the lush green grass and heather on the brae. Closer to the view, a young woman dressed in court's day gown and tall, cone-shaped hat walked along the path. She clutched her wee bairn to her chest while she walked purposefully toward the castle.

The maiden glanced anxiously over her shoulder. She thought she'd heard a sound from behind her. Yet, no one seemed to be around. She hastened her steps. Without warning, a man rushed out of the bushes and snatched the bairn from her arms! The woman found herself on hands and knees in the dirt while the villain escaped.

The castle's beauty belied its dark history, as well as the sinister relationships within. At a precipice atop the spiral stone staircase, an angry male figure argued with the maid. Then in such a heated state, he back-handed her across the face. Her youthful form tumbled backward and down yielding a blood-curdling scream, her face contorted in disbelief. Finally, she lay in a broken heap at the end of the castle stairs.

The Shamanic journey over, Kathy Graves slowly gave herself and the client several moments to return to present time. Through the use of her Reiki talents and Shamanic teachings, Kathy was able to connect the woman with past-life trauma and to offer answers to current relationship difficulties.

Knightmare

The wailing of the siren preceded the careening police car down 42nd Street, barely missing the kids playing stick ball. Officer Larue yelled, "What kind o' call did ya say it was?"

Jones, his buddy, replied, "I dunno for sure. Some messy business on 45th Street. The landlady found the guy; says he's cut pretty bad. She's hysterical; mentioned something about a suit of armor."

Larue jerked the car to a halt in front of the stucco where the call had originated. Jones leapt up the steps and in the door ahead of Larue. He'd just reached the door when Jones poked his head out. "Man, I've never seen anything like this before."

His partner, who'd been on the streets years longer, had seen some pretty bad scenes. He mentally braced himself for another one, shoving his way past Jones. The front door opened into the immaculately kept living room. Then he strode into the dining room; the sight was more than he could handle. He backed out, clutching at his stomach and wretching.

Paul Larue's family had immigrated into America from Ireland only one generation previous to his birth. They were accustomed to bloody violence in the streets of their home country. By moving to the United States, the Larues had hoped to escape the darkness and start a new life. It had not been his parents' intention that Paul would have to participate in scenes such as this in his lifetime.

Glen sat transfixed in front of the black and white set watching an old Superman program. He had no idea what was on though. The only picture in his mind was the one he had seen in Paul's apartment. "All that blood, all that gore, why did you have to check on him? Why couldn't you leave things alone?" he kept reminding himself. Now, all he could do was wait - wait for the police to visit and question. Paul had been his best friend. He mentally rehearsed Paul's story—the one he would have to tell the police.

Sadly, the knight in arms gazed back at me. Something in those void sockets made me catch my breath. A flash of déja vu? Getting a firmer grip on the frame lest I falter, I gingerly hung the parchment at the head of my dining room table where it would begin its necromantic vigil.

From the moment I first spotted it, I knew it was mine. The brass rubbing of the 15th century knight had been shown in the art shop only one day before I bought it. "Hi, Mr. Peterson," I yelled. I had known the owner of the shop for years. I had strained my bank account on several occasions from buying here.

He was a nervous, encyclopedia on art. "Hello, Paul. How goes it today? Anything special? I saw you gazing at the English parchment." Fidgeting more than usual, Peterson straightened a stack of papers on the counter.

"Yeah, I was rather wondering about it." I was lying through my teeth; I was attracted to it and wanted it. "What do you know about it?"

Peterson flinched when I questioned him. His eyes danced from me to the etching just long enough to acknowledge its presence. "I don't know much about it. All I can tell is that it was taken from a figure on a tomb, probably one in an old cathedral. I've seen a few done like that; tourists enjoy doing them. It's been outlawed now though. There is something unusual about this fella though. His sword and spurs are broken. Peterson quickly turned away, hoping to finalize the conversation as if he'd already revealed too much.

But I wasn't so easily put off. "How did you get your hands on it?"

"To tell you the truth, Paul, I don't remember exactly. I was recently cleaning out the attic when I found it stashed away in a corner.

It's been years since I cleaned out parts of that room. I don't recall ever seeing the thing before." Peterson looked at me curiously, "Why're you so interested in it anyway? I'll let you have it reasonably. What is your offer?" He suddenly realized how anxious he was to get rid of the thing; the truth was it actually gave him the creeps.

Less $50, I thanked him and departed. He waved farewell as he held the door for me. If only I had known what he was musing to himself—why he had neglected to tell me that the figure had been completely free of dust when he "discovered" it in the attic after a siege of nightmares.

"It's only my nerves," he decided. "I work too hard. Besides, Paul seemed happy to have it." He was relieved of his qualms about sending the picture to its new home.

Alone with the charcoaled image in my apartment, I felt an uncanny magnetism toward it. He wore such a melancholy expression, and the broken spurs and sword fascinated me. As the evening grew shorter, I tore myself away from my new possession. I locked up for the evening, completing my nightly routine. After a hot shower, I explored the fridge for the milk. I sauntered into the dining room and toasted my companion goodnight. Did I see a mischievous smirk on his face or was it my imagination? It vanished as quickly as it appeared.

After my sojourn that night, I wasn't sure. I awakened about 4:00 AM to heraldry of tournaments and jousts. The dream was still with me fussily in parts. At least, it seemed it was a dream. My body ached from the leaden mail and armor of a knight in duel. I could visualize the colour and pomp of the festivities. It seemed so real. I lay awake a bit longer before falling asleep again, safely not to dream of crashing horses and bodies.

That morning I prepared for work making tea and munching a donut. Flipping on the early news I glanced at the new picture. "Morning, Geoffrey." It popped out so naturally.

Eventually, I was situated at work. "Good morning, Paul," Glen greeted me.

"Hi, Glen," I murmured.

"Boy, you're subdued," he expected an explanation.

I offered little for the time being. "Yeah, I didn't sleep well last night." That was all I was willing to reveal at first; then I gradually recounted the events surrounding the purchase of the picture. "Why don't you stop by for a drink after work? You can take a look at it at the same time."

"Sure, I'm curious. See ya then." Glen went on about his chores, leaving me to concentrate on work.

Later that afternoon, we met at my apartment. "Make yourself at home; what would you like to drink, Glen?"

"The usual." He'd already found the picture and was walking over to it. "Good heavens! It's about to fall off the wall!"

From the bar, I looked to see what he meant. It didn't appear to have slipped; instead, it seemed to have twisted sideways. I had an instantaneous flash from my nightmare. The crash and clamour of armor and my aches from a fall from my mount were renewed.

I must have looked the part too; Glen shook me, "What's wrong? You look terrible!"

Haltingly, I described my dream to Glen. "I can't get rid of it. It's so damned real. I feel like I knew this guy once. I even named him Geoffrey."

"Geoffrey, eh?" Glen slurped the rest of his drink down. "That's quite a story. Wonder what he died of?"

"Stop joking, Glen, it's creepy."

"Don't be so touchy. It's just a picture. I need to get home anyway. Thanks for the drink." Glen started toward the door.

"You're right. Sorry, I'm so jumpy. I don't know why I'm so sensitive toward it. See ya tomorrow." I followed him to the door.

After he'd left, I was still resentful of his flippancy. But, I had other things to do than worry. Changing to jeans and tee-shirt, I settled down to work I'd let slide that afternoon.

Lack of sleep finally wore me down and I began dreaming. I was at battle with bodies of comrads strewn about in a blood bath. I was there to champion my king. My steed stamped restlessly. I heard the unoiled creak of mail in time to see a foe's sword arching toward my throat.

I jerked awake then. Nervous and thirsty, I staggered to the kitchen for water and glanced at the time—6:00 AM. I had to pass the picture on the way.

Then I took a second look - a smudge in the charcoal. I touched it ever so lightly; but it didn't smear further. "Maybe it was there all the time," I muttered slowly.

Shaken and unnerved, I headed for the shower. "These dreams have got to stop." I nearly dropped the glass still in my hand. My hands were trembling.

Later at work, Glen approached me, "You don't look so good, my friend. What's the problem?"

"I'm not sleeping well. I fell asleep shortly after you left yesterday, but I'm having the craziest nightmares." I purposefully omitted the details of the smudge in the charcoal.

Glen shook his head in disbelief. "You say this all started when you bought the picture?"

"I'm afraid so. They're getting worse too. I never used to remember dreams, but these are different, as though I was actually there."

"Paul, I have a friend who is at the University doing some re-search on dreaming. I'd like to give him a call this evening to see what he says about this. Would you like to talk to him?"

"Okay by me." I was curious and scared too.

By the end of the day, I was beat; I felt so tired that I felt as though I had been drugged. I trudged the half mile home, wondering if I would ever make it. Finally entering my apartment, I collapsed on the sofa.

Slowly, I rose from deep fathoms barely to the surface of con-sciousness. I struggled against the embraces of the unknown. I wanted desperately to awaken; instead, I passed on to a separate realm. That which was strange at first, gradually became recognizable and famil-iar.

Eduard, my page, was handing me my armor. "I say, Geoffrey, ye seem engrossed in thought. You're not co-operating with Eduard; ye'll miss the ceremonies. Does Lady Eveline weigh so heavily on your mind?" Henri, my companion, passed through curtained arches to reveal himself.

"Ah, My Friend, still your biting self. Ye'd think I might be spared such pryings on this special day." With this, I dismissed Eduard. "Thank ye; that's all."

Henri admired my garb. "Ye seem quite the admirable figure. Ye shall need it too. Everyone at Court knows of Lady Eveline's escapade."

I defended my honour, "Henri, I was in meditation! She approached so suddenly; I was caught unaware! How I was I to know her intentions? Sir James saw her just as she threw herself upon me. What was I to do? She is promised in marriage to Sir James, but she wants no part of it. She approached me for help. Today of all days, I am to be Knighted and presented at Court. Sir James is favored by the King; I should be lucky to keep my life!"

"It sounds like a likely story. At least I believe you. The Lady's reputation isn't so pure, besides. But, Sir James of all to enrage!" Henri turned his attention to the festivities beyond the open window. We were in a small turret of the castle overlooking the King's Court. Tomorrow I would claim a larger suite as King's liege.

Suddenly there was a signal from the archway. All was ready. Henri directed his gaze at me. "Enough for now; we'll discuss it later." He passed through the archway leaving me to follow.

Each squire to be Knighted made the walk alone to the King's Court. Everyone of consequence had taken their attendance with the King and Queen. That is, all but one. I rounded the passageway to squarely face a formidable, towering suit of armor and blade.

Larue listened to Glen's story and considered how gullible he was. But he was puzzled. Hanging on the wall was a guilt-framed parchment, vacant, holding vigil over the mangled, bloodied body of Paul. Shaking his head and sobbing, Glen repeated in incredulity, "It's awful. It's as though he shrank to fit the suit of armor!"

Larue and Jones looked again at Paul's body, the broken sword held high over his head as though attempting to fend off his attacker. Jones broke the silence, "There's not a drop of blood on his sword. We'll have a time explaining this one."

*Twenty-one years after Knightmares, the identity was learned
of the mysterious brass rubbing. The rubbing of Sir Anthony
de Grey, 1480, can be found in St. Albans Abbey Church,
Herts. This armor is the Richard III style.*

Afterword

All the unfinished business, stories and pieces of a lifetime all gather in a very intense way, particularly if the death is traumatic, to be passed on. These residual fragments do not disperse at death. Instead they find their way into new personalities to sit there, not just in the unconscious but in the physical body.

A remarkable thing happens. When we truly begin to contact the story, the reformation of the story starts to generate energy. It's as though the old life force that was in the old body is coming back again. And when the story starts to surface again with all its energy, the energy is now available to work with. Recent cancer research is showing that some forms can be prevented and/or healed through the identification and integration of these residual fragments.

The ancient Celts believed in reincarnation—the act of becoming born again. They also believed in a metamorphosis or the changing of physical form, as well as metempsychosis—the passing from one body to another after death. These remain possibilities.

Millions of Celtic Souls are realizing and reclaiming themselves today.

However, whether we believe in reincarnation or not is not necessarily important. What we do constructively with the information which presents itself is important. Our own Federal government is involved in research on Inherited Memory, or the "mind of the cells," as a holistic practitioner to alternative medicine would call it. This is the information from all of our ancestors before us which we carry within us.

After all, we are NEVER truly alone. Or as Edgar Cayce put it, "we are the sum total of everything before us and all the experiences of our ancestors." As these experiences are explored, the individual is capable of eliminating those restrictions which we allow to limit our FREEDOM.

Several times as Kimberly typed on the manuscript for "Warrior Poets and Warrior Saints," the computer printed erratically. Still, she tried to ignore the energy coming through the text. Then as she neared completion, one evening the computer switched to a series of ancient symbols and ancient text in script - none of which her machine was 'capable' of creating.

Logic dictated that the computer must have a virus. The printer wouldn't even print the material. One entire screen was full of "y"s written in old script. So, to the repairman or computer doctor went the machine. Everything was fine - diagnosis showed no virus. Of course, her computer operated perfectly on any other documents.

However, as I examined deeper the symbols of Freemasonry and the Knights Templar, the ancient handwritings appearing on her screen, comparing all together I realized that they were from the same source.

Einstein theorized that "time" was merely various layers of energy and space which have yet to be explored. Wolf in his book *Parallel Universes* addressed the same issue of numerous realities existing in and occupying the same space simultaneously.

Arthur Conan Doyle is primarily remembered to us as the creator of Sherlock Holmes. Also, this same sage devoted his life "to giving man the strongest of all reasons to believe in spiritual immortality of the soul, to break down the barrier of death, to found the great religion of the future". In his book *The History of Spiritualism*, Conan Doyle does exactly that.

Another great writer of her time, Adela Rogers St. Johns worked as journalist for the San Francisco "Examiner" and later for the Hearst newspapers. Eventually, she undertook an extensive study of the phenomenon of life beyond death and became convinced that is was no miracle at all, but a realistic experience for everyone. *No Good-byes* was Ms. St. John's book of this proof before she too "crossed over".

It is my observation through years of research, that more people collectively are having these sightings with more detailed interactions among the spirits. Indeed, these areas are the untapped "frontiers" to be explored.

References

Atkin, Malcolm. *The Battle of Worchester, 1651*. Staunton, Virginia: Museum of American Frontier Culture, 1997.

Barrow, G.W.S. *Robert Bruce and the Community of the Realm of Scotland*. Edinburgh, Scotland: Edinburgh Univ. Press, 1965.

———. *The Kingdom of the Scots*. London, England: Edward Arnold Publ., 1973.

Boyter, Ian. *Culloden, The Swords and the Sorrows*. Glasgow, Scotland: The National Trust for Scotland Trading Co., 1996.

Brooks, Janice Y.. *Kings and Queens—The Plantagenets of England*. New York: Thomas Nelson Publ., 1975.

Cage, R.A., Ed.. *The Scots Abroad*. London, England: Croom Helm, 1985.

Costain, Thomas B. *Three Edwards*. New York: Doubleday and Co., 1958.

Coutts, Rev. Alfred. *The Knights Templar in Scotland*. Bruceton Mills, West Va: Unicorn Limited.

Danielewski, John G. *Loch Lomond in Old Picture Postcards*. Zaltbommel, The Netherlands: European Library, 1987.

Davis, I.M. *The Black Douglas*. London, England: Routledge and Kegan Paul, 1974.

Foster, Sally M. *Picts, Gaels, and Scots*. London, England: B.T. Batsford Ltd., 1996.

Glover, Janet R. *The Story of Scotland*. New York: Roy Publ., 1958.

Gray, D.J. *William Wallace: the King's Enemy*. London, England: Robert Hale Ltd. , 1991.

Hunter, James. *A Dance Called America*. Edinburgh, Scotland: Mainstream Publ., 1994.

Kennedy, Frances H., Ed. *The Civil War Battlefield Guide*. Boston: Houghton Mifflin Co., 1990.

Knight, Christopher and Lomas, Robert. *The Hiram Key*. London, England: Century Publ., 1996.

Laing, Lloyd and Jenny. *The Picts and the Scots*. Dover, New Hampshire: Alan Sutton Publ., 1993.

MacKenzie, Agnes M. *Robert Bruce, King of Scots*. Edinburgh, Scotland: Oliver and Boyd Ltd. 1956.

MacLean, Fritzroy. *Highlanders: A History of the Scottish Clans*. New York: Viking Studio Books of Penguin Press, 1995.

MacSween, Anne and Sharp, Mick. *Prehistoric Scotland*. London, England: B.T. Batsford, 1989.

McKnight, W. Mark. "Yankee in Kilts," *Civil War Times Magazine*. New York, 1996.

Magner, Blake A. *Traveller and Company*. Gettysburg, Pennsylvania: Farnsworth House Impressions, 1995.

Matthews, Caitlin. *The Celtic Tradition*. Rockport, Massachusetts: Element Books Ltd., 1995

Miller, Hugh. *Scenes and Legends of the North of Scotland*. Cincinnati, Ohio: Anderson Publ., 1851.

Mitchison, Rosalind. *A History of Scotland*. London, England: Methuen and Co., 1970.

Moncreiffe, Ian and Hicks, David. *The Highland Clans*. London, England, Barrie and Rockliff Publ., 1967.

Murray, W.H. *Rob Roy MacGregor*. Edinburgh, Scotland: Canongate Press Ltd., 1993.

Newton, Toyne with Walker, Charles and Brown, Alan. *The Demonic Connection*. Dorset, England: Blandford Press, 1987.

Palin, Michael. *Palin's Progress and Glen of Weeping* (video). Glencoe, Argyll: Glencoe Productions, 1996.

Palsson, Hermann and Edwards. Paul *Magnus' Saga*. Oxford, England: The Perpetua Press, 1987.

Paterson, Raymond C. *For the Lion*. Edinburgh, Scotland: John Donald Publ., 1996.

Pine, L.G. *The Highland Clans*. Newton Abbot, England: David and Charles Publ., 1972.

Prebble, John. *The Highland Clearances*. London, England: Martin Secker and Warbury Ltd., 1963.

———. *Glencoe: The Story of the Massacre*. New York: Holt, Rinehart and Winston, 1966.

Prebble, John. *The Highland Clearances*. London, England: Martin Secker and Warbury Ltd., 1963.

Reese, Peter. *Wallace: A Biography*. Edinburgh, Scotland: Canongate Books, 1996.

Scott, Ronald McNair. *Robert the Bruce, King of Scots*. New York: Carrole and Graf Publ., 1982

Seagrave, Seija, Ph.D., Ed. *The History of the Irish Brigade*. Fredericksburg, VA: Sergeant Kirkland's Museum and Historical Society Publ., 1997.

Skene, William F. *Celtic Scotland*. Edinburgh, Scotland: David Douglas Publ., 1877.

Southwick, Thomas P. *A Duryee Zouave*. Brookneal, VA: Patrick Schroeder Publ., 1995.

Tabraham, Chris and Fiona Stewart. *Urquhart Castle*. Edinburgh, Scotland: Historic Scotland Publ., 1991.

Thomson, Oliver and MacInnes. *Glencoe*. Edinburgh, Scotland: Howie and Seath Ltd., 1994.

Tranter, Nigel *The Bruce Trilogy*. London, England: Coronet Books of Hodder and Stoughton Ltd., 1969.

Tranter, Nigel. *The Wallace*. London, England: Coronet Books of Hodder and Stoughton Ltd., 1975.

Trout, Robert J. *They Followed the Plume*. Mechanicsburg, Pennsylvania: Stackpole Books, 1993.

Wallace, Randall. *Braveheart*. New York: Pocket Books of Simon and Schuster, 1995.

Ward, Geoffrey C. with Burns, Ric and Ken. *The Civil War*. New York: Alfred A. Knopf, 1990.

Whyte, Donald. *Scottish Surnames and Families*. New York: Barnes and Noble Books, 1996.

For futher Information

Kathy Graves
(Shamanic journeying
and Reiki)
P.O. Box 584
New Plymouth, NJ 07748

Frank Belluardo
(Clan Stevenson)
132 Carr Hollow Rd.
Elizabethton, TN 37643

Dale Shinn
(Functional Period Replica
Firearms & accoutrements)
(Cpt. Jaymes Shinnes Free
Artillery Companie)
P.O. Box 60554
Sacramento, CA 95860

Museum of American Frontier
Culture
P.O. Box 810
Staunton, VA 24402

About the Author

Nannette Morrison is a writer and an Alternative Medicine prac-titioner. She is also a member of Clan Morrison Society.

In her work she practices past-life therapy, massage, Integrative Breathwork, Jin Shin Do, Biomagnetic Therapy, and is a Reiki Master. Ms. Morrison also lectures and teaches classes Reiki, and Bioenergy and Breathwork Therapy. Her research into "Life after Death" and "Near Death Experiences" has extended through many years.

Ms. Morrison is the author of two other books. *Echoes of Valor,* published in 1994, is the result of research with Civil War reenactors having incredible encounters with spirits remaining from that war. Several photographs of these soldiers are captured on film.

A Thundering Silence was published in 1995 as a sequel to the previous book. It also reports on the spirits, past-life experiences and "rescue work" offered.

She may be contacted through her business: Encore Effects, Charlottesville, VA, (804) 293-9650.